Do We Still Need
ST PAUL?

A Contemporary Reading of the Apostle

Do We Still Need
ST PAUL?

A Contemporary Reading of the Apostle

Kieran J. O'Mahony OSA

VERITAS

DEDICATION

First published 2009
Revised 2012
Veritas Publications
7–8 Lower Abbey Street
Dublin 1
Ireland
Email publications@veritas.ie
Website www.veritas.ie

ISBN 978 1 84730 236 6

10 9 8 7 6 5 4 3 2

Chapter 6, 'The Cross in Paul's Vision of Faith', originally appeared in *Bible et Terre Sainte* (José Enrique Aguilar Chiu, Kieran J. O'Mahony and Maurice Roger, eds), Peter Lang Publishing, 2008. Chapter 10, 'Paul as Pastor', originally appeared in *Doctrine and Life*, 55, 2005. Chapter 13, 'Where To From Here', originally appeared in *Doctrine and Life*, 60, 2010. Appendix, 'Paul and Inclusion: Racism Today', originally appeared as 'There is No Distinction – Inclusion in Paul' in *Responding to Racism: A Challenge and a Task for the Catholic Community*, Irish Commission for Justice and Peace, 2001.
Scripture quotations taken from the *New Revised Standard Version Bible*, copyright © 2006 by the National Council of the Churches of Christ in the United States of America.

Cover image © www.imagefile.ie

Printed in the Republic of Ireland
by Gemini International, Dublin

Veritas books are printed on paper made from the wood pulp of managed forests. For every tree felled, at least one tree is planted, thereby renewing natural resources.

ACKNOWLEDGEMENTS

Earlier versions of Chapters 6 and 10 and the appendix, 'Paul and Inclusion: Racism Today' have been published previously and, with some expansion and revision, are offered here with the permission of the publishers involved. Other material was aired in Advent 2008 as part of the 'Word on Web' on-line teaching initiative, in conjunction with Seán Goan, and finds its way into printed format for the first time (www.wordonweb.org). I would like to thank all who took part for their comments and questions.

Some words of gratitude are in order. Gratitude first to the Paul scholars who have inspired me as teachers and friends: Silverio Zedda SJ (Gregorian University, Rome), Jean-Noël Aletti SJ (Pontifical Biblical Institute, Rome), Jerome Murphy-O'Connor OP (École Biblique et Archéologique Française, Jerusalem) and Paolo Garuti OP (École Biblique et Archéologique Française, Jerusalem).

As a lecturer in St Paul at the Milltown Institute of Theology and Philosophy, conversation with students, both undergraduate and postgraduate, challenges me as a teacher and inspires me in my own continued reflection and research. It really is true that the best way to learn is to teach.

Talking to adult faith groups and gatherings of clergy is both a duty and a delight. It is a duty to bring fresh understandings of the Bible beyond the academy and into everyday life. It is also a delight, opening up the issues of today and trying to look at them in fresh ways inspired by the teaching of the apostle. Not least, living and working in the Orlagh Retreat Centre brings many opportunities, formal and informal, to speak about the Pauline letters and their continued potential today.

'Thanks be to God for his indescribable gift!'
(2 Corinthians 9:15)

CONTENTS

	Introduction	11
CHAPTER 1	Do We Still Need St Paul?	13
CHAPTER 2	St Paul the Letter-Writer	23
CHAPTER 3	The Laity, the Church and St Paul	33
CHAPTER 4	Why did Paul Persecute Christians?	42
CHAPTER 5	The Conversion of St Paul	51
CHAPTER 6	The Cross in Paul's Vision of Faith	57
CHAPTER 7	Why is Easter at the Centre?	65
CHAPTER 8	St Paul and Suffering	75
CHAPTER 9	Prayer in the Spirit	88
CHAPTER 10	Paul as Pastor	103
CHAPTER 11	St Paul and the Lord's Supper	120
CHAPTER 12	Women in the Pauline Assemblies	130
CHAPTER 13	Where to From Here?	138
	Conclusion	149
APPENDIX	Paul and Inclusion: Racism Today	153
	Suggested Further Reading	172
	Index of Biblical Citations	174
	Index of non-Biblical Citations	179

INTRODUCTION

This book is intended to bring forward the understanding of the interested believer, who has already gained some familiarity with the life and times of St Paul. It looks at the formative experiences of Paul, the foundation stones of his great teaching about Jesus, his cross and resurrection, to see if we today can learn from those ground-breaking experiences and reflections. It is about the *religious ideas* or theology of Paul. At the same time, an eye is kept on the contemporary situation of faith and Church. These essays are thus an *applied reading* of Paul.

The first chapter addresses the question posed by the book's title and looks at ways in which we still need Paul today. Following on that is a chapter which touches on the letter-writing techniques evident in these documents. It explores how speech patterns from the period had their influence especially on the layout of the letters. The rhetorical structure does enable a clearer reading of the arguments presented. Chapter 3 reflects on the context of Church today and asks if our biblical resources, in particular Paul, can be of help to us. The next four chapters form a kind of unity and the topics, as the reader will notice immediately, are distinguishable but not separable. Why Paul persecuted Christians forms the essential background to his new understanding of the cross in the light of his encounter with Christ risen. Here, in my view, is great potential for today, as we search again for new language for all that God has done for us in Jesus. Chapters 8 and 9 follow closely because they attempt to portray Paul's personal appropriation of the Christ event, especially in his own prayer and suffering. A very human Paul emerges here. The previous chapters prepare us for a portrayal of

Paul as pastor – what was his style and can we be inspired today by him? We can see him as pastor as he addresses the issue of the Lord's Supper in Corinth. Finally, two topics are raised which are of contemporary relevance. It is often felt that Paul is somehow against women, so Chapter 12 explores the role of women in the Pauline communities. The last chapter offers a Pauline reading of the future of the Church in the light of the abuse crisis. After the conclusion, there is an appendix which uses insights from St Paul to reflect on racism today. Racism is a constant risk as society becomes more multicultural and the risk is even greater in a time of economic downturn. The inclusive teaching of the letter to the Romans can speak to us all today. I also include in the appendix a previously published chapter which deals with the issue of racism. The risk of racism is ever-present, especially in societies that are increasingly multi-cultural, and especially at times of economic downturn. The inclusive teaching of the letter to the Romans has potential to speak to us today as believers and unbelievers.

My hope is that new inspiration can be found through St Paul's letters to take up again the challenge of the Good News in Christ.

Chapter 1

DO WE STILL NEED ST PAUL?

In celebrating the Year of St Paul, the second reading at Sunday Mass may at last be the inspiration of the homily. It is natural, of course, that the Gospel narrative should draw the attention of both hearer and speaker because it is through the essential nature of story that the reader is drawn in. Nevertheless, to neglect the earliest and perhaps the mightiest Christian writer would seem to be an unnecessary deprivation.

It is not that there are no problems with the excerpts read in the liturgy. First, the short selections come from long, often complex mosaics of persuasion, and just as the pieces in a real mosaic make sense only when we see the full picture, likewise the excerpts find their meaning in the context of longer reflections. Second, Paul is difficult, as was noted very early on in the tradition: 'So also our beloved brother Paul wrote to you according to the wisdom given him, speaking of this as he does in all his letters. There are some things in them hard to understand' (2 Pet 3:15-16). Indeed there are! So, do we still need St Paul today? Let me outline why I think he is still an essential guide to the Christian life, a resource for today who can inspire and inform.

1. RELIGIOUS EXPERIENCE

In the West at least, the mainline Christian churches are in rapid recession. The one exception is the dramatic rise of the Pentecostalist movement(s). One of the reasons, surely, is that the Pentecostalist churches give significant space to religious experience and are not afraid of the emotional dimension of believing and worshipping, whereas all the churches of the West have had their reservations about 'religious experience'. Perhaps one of the reasons for church decline is simply that there is little in people's experience that corresponds with the wonderful proclamation and promise of the Good News. There are two gaps in reality. There is the gap between what is proclaimed and how people experience their world. The gap between head and heart is sustained by the dry didacticism of much common worship.

In some contrast, St Paul was first and foremost someone utterly swept away by his *experience* of the risen Lord. As a zealously observant Jew, he was always a person of prayer. The big 'turning' in his life occurred because of a revelation, as he tells us: 'But when God … was pleased to reveal his Son to me' (Gal 1:15-16). He had other religious experiences, which he narrates with convincing reluctance in 2 Corinthians 12. In the letter to the Galatians, in a unique personal note, he tells us: 'And the life I now live in the flesh I live by the faith of the Son of God, *who loved me* and gave himself *for me*' (Gal 2:20; emphasis added). To use his own words, nothing could ever separate him from the love of God, revealed in Christ Jesus our Lord (Rom 8:39). Although a great teacher of *faith* precisely as faith, in some sense or other, Paul also *knew* the truth of the Gospel, and for him it was not a speculation but a fact, a fact of experience, the reality of the Risen Lord, the reality of being loved to such an extraordinary, hardly believable extent.

Perhaps here for us today is an invitation to give great importance to the experiential and emotional dimensions of believing. The regeneration of the Church, if it is to happen, can have no other genesis, if not in the heart and mind of the believer. Otherwise, we run the risk of passing on the faith 'second-hand', as a kind of commodity, rather than a relationship.

2. MINISTRY

Ministry in the mainline churches is also undergoing a crisis. Is it imaginable that we, at such a distance in time and culture, could learn today from someone who lived so long ago? A good place to begin might be Paul's own pastoral practice.

After two thousand years of Church it can be difficult to conjure up the earliest experience of ministry, which must have been significantly different. What happened when St Paul arrived in a new city, for instance in Thessalonica? How did he start? How did he convince? A reconstruction is not easy to arrive at, but a clue may be found in an unusual, even daring, expression that he uses in his writings: 'Be imitators of me, as I am of Christ' (1 Cor 11:1; cf. also 1 Cor 4:16; 1 Thess 1:6; 2 Thess 3:7, 9; Gal 4:12). The sequence is striking, because he puts himself between the believer and Christ. I understand this to mean that Paul could not simply *tell* people about the Good News in Christ. In order that they might sense it or feel it as something genuine and real, he would have had to model the Good News for them in his person and in his behaviour. Paul – so much *against* any vaunting of self – is not boasting when he says, 'Be imitators of me, as I am of Christ'. He is simply describing his actual ministry, as an elderly confrère of mine used to put it, 'in all humility, but with an emphasis on the truth'! It is not too much to say that Paul had to *be* what he proclaimed; otherwise it would have been mere words. Naturally, there is more to it than that, but we have touched on something very alive and central: bearers of the Good News who are themselves being transformed by the Gospel have a persuasive force that no mere doctrinal exhortation, however brilliant, can match.

This, in turn, does raise a question about the core of ministry in our own day. Unless the bearer of the Good News is *being transformed* by what he or she proclaims, the word will be stillborn. The increasing professionalisation of ministry, among both clergy and pastoral agents, may be necessary, but it does also risk being beside the point. In the end, we are looking for Christ-like figures, people who convince first by who they are and what they do even before they speak. This is no doubt a very demanding, even impossible ideal, but should any of us be satisfied with less? Perhaps the now-distant ministry of Paul, apparently so remote, can bring us nearer to the heart of proclamation in our own time and place. The conviction of convinced believers has its own persuasive power.

3.   Trusting his hearers

The loudest complaint among those still going to church is about the quality of homilies. It is no secret that a renewal of preaching did not accompany the renewal of the liturgy after Vatican II. It is not that we lack for resources: never were more books, commentaries, internet articles and the like at our disposal. It is even said that Ireland has the highest per priestly capita sales on books of homilies and about preaching. Nevertheless, preaching remains unexcited and unexciting – curious in a country renowned for the agility of its language.

It is worth asking how this has come about. I suspect we have been betrayed by two trends in the last thirty or forty years of preaching. The first trend is to have 'one idea', leading to the gross simplification of the Christian project. Christianity doesn't have to be impenetrably complicated, but it *is* complex. Listening to much preaching, one might be justified in concluding that there isn't actually a whole lot to Christianity. It is not that a return to the catechism preaching of a more theological bent is the solution, but rather that an appropriate depth of analysis and richness of proclamation are necessary if we are to speak to the educated people of today. The second debilitating trend is to make morals the connecting point with people's lives. This is both easy and fatal. It is *easy*, in that none of us is perfect and so something along of the lines of 'therefore let us be better' will always hit home. But bear in mind that people, being told they should be better, also feel assessed and judged. As a result, often their heads are with us, but not their hearts. It is *fatal* because morality is not at the centre of the Christian proclamation. It is Christ who is the centre and we behave in distinctive ways as a response to Christ. Can we learn from St Paul – who candidly confirms the assessment of the Corinthians: 'His letters are weighty and strong, but his bodily presence is weak, and his speech contemptible' (2 Cor 10:10)? There may be encouragement there for people who don't feel up to public speaking and preaching!

St Paul regularly trusts his audience with the strong meat of his deepest convictions. The apostle always *persuades*, that is, he lines up real arguments in structured sequence, hoping to move by reasoned conviction, not by sheer force. Perhaps the most daunting, yet illuminating example of this approach is the whole letter to the Romans. Paul honours his hearers and readers (then and now), by offering us complex reflections on complex issues and by *not* making things apparently easy that in reality are difficult. He does, of course, give advice – moral, spiritual and practical. But the advice is always in light of the Gospel, the Christ event. Nowhere is this clearer than in the first letter to the Corinthians. This letter contains a great deal of advice, but the advice is framed by the Cross (1 Cor 1) and the Resurrection (1 Cor 15). These are the bookends of the Christian proclamation, so that whatever advice is given is held up by the core reality of what God has done for us in Jesus.

Is there not something to be learned here for our preaching today? Should we not show the same joyful seriousness and depth? Can we not trust our hearers – or is it ourselves? – with the strong meat of deep conviction and effective persuasion? It is true that congregations are always mixed and to some extent we have to choose a level on which to speak. But why choose always the lowest common denominator? The educated believers of today are ready for something more substantial and engaging, something more challenging, and in the end something more life-giving.

4. CHRIST

Even though Christ is at the centre, there are two tremendous challenges to Christian faith today closely connected to our faith in Jesus. The first is the awareness of all the other possible faiths in the world, an awareness that can lead to a feeling that all religions are essentially the same. Was there really anything so special about Jesus? The second question is internal to our faith: we are not sure how to talk today about God in Christ and Christ on the cross. In technical terms, we have not found a contemporary language to talk about the incarnation (Jesus as both human and divine) and redemption (what happened in his death and resurrection for us). These topics cannot be said to be on the periphery. As part of the task of finding new language, we can revitalise our perspectives by dialogue with the 'greats' who were there at the start, pre-eminently among them, Saul who became Paul.

As you will have noticed, the religious experience of Paul was the risen Lord, simply. When he proclaimed, he spoke from within his own experience of being transformed by Christ, 'who loved me and gave himself for me'. In his persuasion, everything comes from and leads to Christ. We too are invited to trust this experience of faith. We are also called to allow ourselves to be loved, even if it is difficult to imagine that the creator of the cosmos could be a lover who comes so close to us in Jesus of Nazareth. We too are invited to let our whole lives and selves be shaped by faith in the Lord Jesus, just as Paul did.

While aware that God is working through all the other faiths, for us Christ stands at the centre. While aware that God is saving through all the other faiths, the cross, paradoxical and radically *different*, is still our turning point in time. The words of the first encyclical of Benedict XVI come to mind: 'Being Christian is not the result of an ethical choice or a lofty idea, but the encounter with an event, a person, which gives life a new horizon and a decisive direction' (*Deus caritas est*, 1). This encounter has the potential to transform our lives, while opening a new horizon of understanding. St Paul expresses it poetically, providing a wonderful summary of his world view:

> But just as we have the same spirit of faith that is in accordance with scripture – 'I believed, and so I spoke' – we also believe, and so we speak, because we know that the one who raised the Lord Jesus will raise us also with Jesus, and will bring us with you into his presence. Yes, everything is for your sake, so that grace, as it extends to more and more people, may increase thanksgiving, to the glory of God. (2 Cor 4:13-15)

DO WE STILL NEED ST PAUL?

We still need St Paul because the 'future Church' will have to be a place of encounter, transformation, passion and understanding. In equal measure we need passionate and intelligent believers, whose being transformed by faith is driven by the encounter with the risen Lord and expressed in reasonable dialogue with the world.

THE YEAR OF PAUL

To bring this invitation to a conclusion, it might help to locate St Paul in the first century of our era. Although this year has been proclaimed the Year of St Paul, to mark the 2,000th anniversary of his birth, in reality no one knows when he was born. The Irish Paul scholar, Jerome Murphy-O'Connor OP, makes a very good case for bringing the birth of Paul back to roughly the same time as Jesus himself, that is 6–4 BC. However, it is possible to establish two dates in the life and ministry of Paul: the date of his conversion and the date of his first stay in Corinth. We shall look at each in turn.

THE CONVERSION OF SAUL

St Paul himself provides an important clue as to the date of his conversion, when he mentions the time he escapes from Damascus. 'In Damascus, the governor under King Aretas guarded the city of Damascus in order to seize me, but I was let down in a basket through a window in the wall, and escaped from his hands' (2 Cor 11:32-33). This rather modest departure is confirmed in the Acts of the Apostles:

> After some time had passed, the Jews plotted to kill him, but their plot became known to Saul. They were watching the gates day and night so that they might kill him; but his disciples took him by night and let him down through an opening in the wall, lowering him in a basket. (Acts 9:23-25)

It so happens that the reign of King Aretas IV over Damascus can be fairly closely dated. To start the story at the right point, it helps to recall that King Aretas has one other important biblical link in the New Testament. One of his daughters was married to the tetrarch Herod Antipas before he divorced her to marry Herodias, the wife of his half-brother Herod Philip. John the Baptist condemned the divorce and was imprisoned, then executed by Herod Antipas around AD 29 (Mt 14:3-12 and par.). Aretas' anger found revenge only later, in AD 36, when he attacked and defeated the army of Herod Antipas, gaining control of Damascus. Tiberius sent Vitellius, the governor of Syria, to punish Aretas for his actions, but the Roman emperor's death in AD 36–37 cancelled the expedition (*Jewish Antiquities* 18.5.1–3 §109–25). Aretas himself died in AD 40. This means that Paul's escape took place in the period AD 36–40.

After Damascus, Paul eventually made what seems to have been a fairly furtive visit to Jerusalem:

> Then after three years I did go up to Jerusalem to visit Cephas and stayed with him fifteen days; but I did not see any other apostle except James the Lord's brother. (Gal 1:18-20)

> When he had come to Jerusalem, he attempted to join the disciples; and they were all afraid of him, for they did not believe that he was a disciple. But Barnabas took him, brought him to the apostles, and described for them how on the road he had seen the Lord, who had spoken to him, and how in Damascus he had spoken boldly in the name of Jesus. So he went in and out among them in Jerusalem, speaking boldly in the name of the Lord. (Acts 9:26-28)

If these two texts both refer to the same journey to Jerusalem, then we can date the conversion of Paul to three years before his escape from Damascus. The conversion could, in that case, have taken place in the period 34–37. From a modern point of view, a three-year time span might seem too broad to be useful, but when we consider that Paul at this stage was still not a figure on the Christian scene, the dating is in fact relatively accurate. A really early date – for instance AD 34 – would raise the intriguing possibility that the arrival of Paul on the scene was quite close to the time of Jesus' death and the very earliest years of the Christian Church. In that year, Paul would have been about forty to forty-two years of age. The great journeys are still a long way in the future, and when he undertook them he was in his middle to late fifties.

VISIT TO CORINTH

The other fairly secure date in Pauline chronology is his first visit to Corinth. In the Acts of the Apostles, a Roman official is mentioned as proconsul in Achaia at the time Paul was there.

> But when Gallio was proconsul of Achaia, the Jews made a united attack on Paul and brought him before the tribunal. They said, 'This man is persuading people to worship God in ways that are contrary to the law'. Just as Paul was about to speak, Gallio said to the Jews, 'If it were a matter of crime or serious villainy, I would be justified in accepting the complaint of you Jews; but since it is a matter of questions about words and names and your own law, see to it yourselves; I do not wish to be a judge of these matters'. And he dismissed them from the tribunal. Then all of them seized Sosthenes, the official of the synagogue, and beat him in front of the tribunal. But Gallio paid no attention to any of these things. (Acts 18:12-17)

By very good fortune, an inscription in Delphi, in central Greece, helps us to date the time when Paul was in Achaia, of which Corinth was the chief city. Paul himself, an insignificant figure to the official world of the time, is not mentioned in the inscription, but Gallio is. His time in office can be deduced from the somewhat fragmentary text, and from that it is possible to narrow down the time Paul was in Corinth to late AD 51 and early AD 52. From this secure date one may calculate backwards and forwards and create at least a relative chronology for the journeys and letter-writing of the middle-aged Paul.

These two dates remind us of just how close Paul was in time to the ministry of Jesus. If the calculation of the conversion has some accuracy, it means the gap in time between Jesus and Paul was only six or eight years. The dating of the time in Corinth takes us to a period before any gospel was written down. In the letters, we have not only the individual voice of the apostle but also the very first documents of Christianity to come down to us. These very first documents are also among the most significant. It was indeed a blessing that so gifted a disciple was available for the apostolate at so formative a stage in the Christian movement. In our own way, we are again at a formative stage. In the following chapters we will use the letters as a resource to interrogate and to reignite our faith and discipleship today.

Chapter 2

ST PAUL THE LETTER-WRITER

It has often been observed that the most common type of document in the New Testament is the letter. Twenty of the twenty-seven documents are letters. There are even letters in the documents that are not in themselves letters, for example in the Acts of the Apostles and in the Book of Revelation. This is all in some contrast with the very first stages of the Christian movement, which operated on an oral level, going back to Jesus himself. The use of this literary form tells us a great deal about the mobility of early Christianity, as it spread across the eastern and later the western Mediterranean. Of the thirteen letters attributed to Paul, the common opinion is that he wrote seven of these. Ordinarily, Titus and 1 and 2 Timothy are held to reflect a later Church context and problematic. There is some discussion about the authenticity of Colossians and Ephesians, though many scholars still think these are Deutero-Pauline, while 2 Thessalonians remains problematic for a variety of reasons. That leaves us with the seven so-called genuine or authentic letters, that is, Romans, 1 and 2 Corinthians, Galatians, Philippians, 1 Thessalonians and Philemon.

In all the talk about Paul, a simple question can be asked: why did Paul write letters? Further questions regard the production, circulation and use of the letters. The answer to the first question is in one sense obvious. Paul wrote letters because he was absent from the communities he founded and wished to be in touch with them. In that sense the letters are part of the missionary strategy of the later, highly mobile Paul. His stated desire is to found as many communities as possible, in the Greco-Roman world, under the pressure of the second coming of Christ.

The importance of the Second Coming of Christ

Paul, who as a Pharisee belonged to an eschatological wing of Judaism, remained an eschatological thinker as a Christian, as is clear from 1 Thessalonians and 1 Corinthians 15. Included in the world view of apocalyptic eschatology was the conviction that God had arranged a day to bring the course of world history to an end when the living and the dead would be judged. The first instalment of this event had already occurred in Jesus' resurrection. Resurrection was viewed as an end-time event, and the totally unexpected anticipation of the end, within history so to speak, in Jesus' resurrection meant that the end had already started and, naturally, would be completed. In part, this accounts for the haste of Paul's final years: he was keen to bring the offer of God's grace to as many as possible before the final curtain.

An immediate consequence of that desire to reach as many as possible is that Paul 'moves on'. He leaves behind a faith community or faith communities, usually with some minimal structure in place ('But we appeal to you, brothers and sisters, to respect those who labour among you, and have charge of you in the Lord and admonish you; esteem them very highly in love because of their work' [1 Thess 5:12-13]). It would seem that Paul's desire to 'move on' was greater than his desire to oversee the faith coming to maturity in a particular place. For instance, in Corinth, he admits himself that he did not trust them with the whole proclamation ('I fed you with milk, not solid food, for you were not ready for solid food' [1 Cor 3:2]). The fact that he did not baptise many in Corinth is a striking example of his pastoral sensitivity to people's readiness for full commitment: 'I thank God that I baptised none of you except Crispus and Gaius, so that no one can say that you were baptised in my name. (I did baptise also the household of Stephanas; beyond that, I do not know whether I baptised anyone else)' (1 Cor 1:14-16).

This desire to keep moving brought with it two risks. The first risk is that someone else could come along and 'complete' the work in a way that was not consistent with Paul's own teaching. This certainly happened in Galatia and perhaps also in Corinth. The second risk was that external and internal pressures might have proved too much for the fledgling communities. Thessalonica and Philippi are examples of places where persecution took place. The internal pressures in Corinth turned out to be enormous, calling for substantial responses over a longer period of time. Finally, the letters are also written in response to specific questions brought to Paul either by someone from the community (Galatians) or by his own representative (Thessalonians, for example).

The letters, then, are an attempt to continue to 'be present' to the communities while physically absent. This fulfils one of the functions of ancient letters that is *parousia*: being present to while actually away. The other functions were friendship (*philosphronesis*) and advice (*omilia*). There is a very touching moment in 1 Thessalonians that illustrates what is meant: 'As for us, brothers and sisters, when, for a short time, we were made orphans by being separated from you – in person, not in heart – we longed with great eagerness to see you face to face' (1 Thess 2:17-18).

THE STRUCTURES OF LETTER-WRITING

Letter-writing, then and now, is highly conventional. We have our conventions today, usually distinguishing personal and professional communications. In Paul's, the structure of a letter was different. For example, instead of starting with the name of the recipient (Dear X), it began with the name of the sender (From X). A typical letter form from the time would look like this:

Introduction	Sender's name, addressee, greetings, and often an additional greeting and wish for good health.
Text or body	Topics would be introduced in a characteristic formula.
Conclusion	This would include greetings again, good wishes, especially for persons other than the addressee; perhaps final greeting or prayer sentence. Rarely is a date given.

An example of such a letter can be found conveniently in the Acts of the Apostles:

> Then the apostles and the elders, with the consent of the whole Church, decided to choose men from among their members and to send them to Antioch with Paul and Barnabas. They sent Judas called Barsabbas, and Silas, leaders among the brothers, with the following letter: 'The brothers, both the apostles and the elders, to the believers of Gentile origin in Antioch and Syria and Cilicia, greetings. Since we have heard that certain persons who have gone out from us, though with no instructions from us, have said things to disturb you and have unsettled your minds, we have decided unanimously to choose representatives and send them to you, along with our beloved Barnabas and Paul, who have risked their lives for the sake of our Lord Jesus Christ. We have therefore sent Judas and Silas, who themselves will tell you the same things by word of mouth. For it has seemed good to the Holy Spirit and to us to impose on you no further burden than these essentials: that you abstain from what has been sacrificed to idols and from blood and from what is strangled and from fornication. If you keep yourselves from these, you will do well. Farewell.' (Acts 15:22-29)

As is well known, Paul made a few adjustments to this outline, the most significant of which is the introduction of an extended thanksgiving at the start of the letters (with the notable exception of Galatians). A short example of the format of a Pauline letter would be the letter to Philemon.

Introduction	Paul and Timothy to Philemon, Apphia and Archippus, and the house Church.
Thanksgiving	This takes up vv.4-7.

DO WE STILL NEED ST PAUL?

Text or body	Various issues are raised in vv.8-18.
Conclusion	Practical arrangements and greetings are contained in vv.9-25.

The passage from the Acts also tells us how private individuals managed to get letters to their desired destinations. There was no system for the distribution of letters, apart from the imperial postage system, which was limited to government functionaries. Ordinarily, if you wanted to send a letter from Alexandria in Egypt to Rome, you had to find someone making that journey across the Mediterranean and then hope they would be able to find the addressee and hand over the letter. Naturally, this was not always successful. The apostles entrusted the letter cited above to specific bearers, who had the additional task of expanding upon and explaining the contents. In the case of Paul, more recent research suggests that he had his own small administrative unit, made up of people he could send to a particular community with the task of elaboration. The example of Timothy being sent to see how the Thessalonians were faring illustrates this system. The letters do sometimes need explanation. (*Somebody* must have explained Galatians to the addresses!) Naturally, an administrative unit, however small, entails expenditure. Timothy would have had to have money for food and lodgings on the way. Given that the Thessalonians were notably poor, Paul may even have preferred that Timothy pay his own way while among them. The urgency and importance of the contents would surely have motivated Paul to make sure by means of a bearer who was also a fellow-worker that his advice really did reach, for example, the Corinthians.

Paul wrote *to persuade,* and it should not surprise that the content of his letters was influenced by the training in speech-making that marked Greco-Roman culture. Today the word 'rhetoric' conjures up the impression of empty show. It was not ever thus.

Because the culture was primarily an oral one, speech-making held an important place in public life. The areas of life particularly affected were politics, law and public celebrations. All three contexts called for persuasive, sometimes celebratory words. Given the power of speeches, it is natural that the school curriculum, such as it was, placed a strong emphasis on preparing the youth to take up roles in public life, primarily as politicians and lawyers. Handbooks were written and published at the time, and indeed, remarkably enough, ten of these handbooks from the time of Paul have survived, both in Greek and in Latin.

The advice in the handbooks, at least in the earliest stages, was descriptive rather than prescriptive. The authors were saying, in effect: this is what works, so far as we can see. (Later on, a scholastic systematisation made the handbooks rather theoretical and prescriptive.) Some of the advice on rhetoric, defined as the art of speaking well, can help in following the arguments in Paul's letters. For example, the Rhetoricians noticed that constructing a speech involved five steps, which can, at least in theoretical reflection, be distinguished. First, the writer had to know what the core issue was and what would be the main or central focus of the speech. Paul does inform himself closely regarding the situation in Corinth, for instance, before making detailed responses. Second, the arguments needed to be placed in the most persuasive sequence. We will see in a moment that Paul does follow the advice on layout in this letter. Third, it was recommended to pay attention to the nature of the argument in each step and the beauty of the presentation. Metaphors, similes and rhythm were all possible embellishments. Fourth and fifth, they advised that you memorise and practice the speech. For the nature of this examination, the last two steps are not relevant, but the first three are. In particular the second step, the persuasive layout, can help a great deal in tracing the sequence of arguments across the letters.

The persuasive layout began very simply: inform them of what you are going to say, and then say it. By the time Paul would have been at school, an elaborate reflection on effective persuasion had evolved. Every persuasion could have up to five distinct sections. A brief word about each step will be in order:

1. The *Introduction* was designed to get the attention and good will of the hearers and make them well disposed towards the speaker.
2. The *Statement of Facts* was essential in a criminal case, because it put before the court the evidence which was to be interpreted by the defence or prosecution. In the case of political or celebratory speeches it was not strictly necessary.
3. The *Thesis*: what the speaker intended to prove. This could have been a single sentence or it might have been divided up into three (but not more!) parts.
4. The various *Proofs* made up the real body of the persuasion and it was possible to use a great variety of arguments – syllogisms, examples from the past, or the good character of the people involved and the like.
5. The *Conclusion* had the function of summing up and synthesising what had been said. It shared with the *Introduction* the function of gaining again the good will of the hearers. It was usually a little more emotional, because what strikes a chord with the heart stays longer in the memory.

This sounds complicated and dry, but in reality it was not first of all theoretical but practical. It arose from the experience of public speaking and from a systematic reflection on 'what worked'. A nice example of such a persuasion can be found in Paul's speech on the Areopagus in Athens (Acts 17:22-31):

> Then Paul stood in front of the Areopagus and said:
>
> *Introduction*
> Athenians, I see how extremely religious you are in every way. For as I went through the city and looked carefully

at the objects of your worship, I found among them an altar with the inscription, 'To an unknown god'.

Thesis
What therefore you worship as unknown, this I proclaim to you.

Proof 1
The God who made the world and everything in it, he who is Lord of heaven and earth, does not live in shrines made by human hands, nor is he served by human hands, as though he needed anything, since he himself gives to all mortals life and breath and all things.

Proof 2
From one ancestor he made all nations to inhabit the whole earth, and he allotted the times of their existence and the boundaries of the places where they would live, so that they would search for God and perhaps grope for him and find him – though indeed he is not far from each one of us. For 'In him we live and move and have our being'; as even some of your own poets have said, 'For we too are his offspring'.

Conclusion
Since we are God's offspring, we ought not to think that the deity is like gold, or silver, or stone, an image formed by the art and imagination of mortals. While God has overlooked the times of human ignorance, now he commands all people everywhere to repent, because he has fixed a day on which he will have the world judged in righteousness by a man whom he has appointed, and of this he has given assurance to all by raising him from the dead.

It is possible to use the same outline to trace the argument across a whole letter in Paul. 1 Thessalonians provides a short example.

Verses	Letter	Speech (Rhetoric)
1:1	Sender and greetings	
1:2-10	Thanksgiving	*Introduction*
1:9-10		*Thesis (in three parts)*
2:1–3:12	Body	*Proof 1: Relationships*
4:1-12		*Proof 2: Holiness*
4:13–5:11		*Proof 3: End-time issues*
5:12-27	Exhortations	*Conclusion*
5:28	Final greeting	

The key really is 1:9-10, which reads:

1:9 For the people of those regions report about us what kind of welcome we had among you	= Proof 1 on relationships
and how you turned to God from idols, to serve a living and true God,	= Proof 2 on how to live a holy life
10 and to wait for his Son from heaven, whom he raised from the dead – Jesus, who rescues us from the wrath that is coming.	= Proof 3 dealing with the end-time issues.

In this way, it is possible to follow the steps of an argument in Paul. The thanksgiving, corresponding to the introduction, has the function of gaining the good will and attention of the recipients. The thesis informs the hearers of the topics to come, then are dealt with in a series of proofs. Finally, the conclusion – expressed in an emotional pile-up of commands – takes us back to the start and offers a quick 'flashback' over the whole persuasion.

Such a combination of letter convention and persuasive underlay may help readers to see that any paragraph from Paul is really only one piece of an elaborate communication and cannot really be grasped as an isolated religious thought or teaching. Instead, like pieces of a mosaic, a paragraph needs to be put back into the whole picture for its true significance to become apparent. Finally, the skill involved here allows us to surmise something about Paul's education, otherwise of course unknown. It is very likely that this skill in communicating is a fruit of sheer natural ability allied to the benefits of a formal Greco-Roman schooling.

Chapter 3

THE LAITY, THE CHURCH AND ST PAUL

In *God's New Man*, Paul Collins reports a standard, if much more skewed than usual, nineteenth-century opinion. Monsignor George Talbot de Malahide, an Anglo-Irish convert to Catholicism and an important figure in the court of Pius IX, once wrote: 'What is the province of the laity? To hunt, to shoot, to entertain? These matters they understand, but to meddle with ecclesiastical matters they have no right at all.' This is an extreme example of a pervasive clericalism which has marked the Church to our own time. Vatican II provided a richer and deeper image: the People of God – a significant choice on account of its biblical inspiration. Historians remind us that the effects of a Church council are felt over decades and even centuries. This would certainly have been the case with earlier gatherings, such as Trent. But in our time, when culture moves forward so rapidly and change turns over so quickly, it is not too much to say that we live now not only forty or fifty years since Vatican II, but also in a different world, externally and internally. Not only has the world experienced profound changes, often summarised by the shorthand expression 'post-modernism', but also the Church has experienced a change without precedent in context and in status. In the case of the Irish Church, we live now in an extraordinary moment: Catholicism still pervades the culture, yet the understanding of the faith (even knowing what you *don't* believe in) is minimal. The self-inflicted wounds of the institution have taken their toll. The parish system is about to undergo what we may call a 'presbyterianisation', as the ordinary membership takes up responsibility for the tasks monopolised by the disappearing clergy. What is to come we do not know, except that we know it can only be the same by becoming very different.

Part of the inheritance of Vatican II was the call to a renewed use of the 'sources' of the faith. Here scripture is our major resource. At the same time, in our particular cultural moment, with all due help from scripture and tradition, we are responsible for what is to be, largely because our world is so entirely different from that of almost all previous Christian generations, and utterly remote from the world of the New Testament.

WHERE SCRIPTURE CAN HELP US

As we saw, the seven authentic letters of Paul constitute the 'archeological' remains of living relationships and of a daring missionary programme. They also offer a remarkable partner in dialogue as we re-vision the Church for the twenty-first century. We can *today* learn these early textual remnants, if I may so describe our inspired scripture. In particular, we can be inspired by Paul the listener (1 Thessalonians), Paul the teacher (Romans) and Paul the community builder and reconciler (1 and 2 Corinthians).

FIRST LETTER TO THE THESSALONIANS

The background to the first letter to the Thessalonians is a combination of anxiety and relief. There is relief and even joy at the time of writing the letter. But before that Paul is not ashamed to confess his anxiety about the capacity of the Thessalonians to withstand persecution, and acknowledges frankly the Thessalonians' own doubts about him. Paul had spent a considerable and intense period in the city and had left behind a vibrant community with some leadership in place. His usual practice of taking no money, his subsequent absence and his later sending of a representative and not going himself gave rise to doubts in the community about his integrity and sincerity. Not only that, they still had questions to ask him about the faith. How does Paul know all this? His messenger Timothy had brought back news of what was going on – not only the specific questions regarding living in a polytheistic, imperial society and the questions about the dead, but also what the Thessalonians were feeling deeply and suspecting. In reality, the first part of the letter is the most carefully written, with a real desire to acknowledge the doubts and difficult experiences of the Thessalonians and also to assure them of real understanding, even a sharing of their experience. It is noticeable that while earlier Paul describes himself as a father to them and even a mother (a wet nurse specifically), in 2:17 he says he feels orphaned from them, in other words he understands their experience *from the inside*.

As a pastor, Paul listened deeply to the Thessalonians, not only paying attention to the presenting issues, which have their own importance, but attending to the inner world of the Thessalonian community. The first part of the letter, which is a succinct history of the relationship, combines affirmation of the Thessalonians and their religious experience with an *apologia* of Paul's ministry among them. *Apologia* is perhaps not quite the right term, because Paul's purpose is not simply to account for himself but to re-establish the relationship with the Thessalonians, in a genuine and life-giving way. It is not simply a matter of explaining, or even worse explaining away his behaviour, but much more: it is a return to that heart-to-heart openess and sincerity which first convinced the Thessalonians. The implications of such a style will be explored when we have looked at other Pauline texts.

LETTERS TO THE ROMANS

As an example of another dimension of listening, I will speak about the letter to the Romans. This exceptional text differs from other Pauline letters in that he is writing to a community of which he is not the 'father' and where he can claim no special authority or relationship. As is well known, the Roman community was divided somewhat along ethnic and religious lines. Those of Gentile origin seem to have looked down on those of Jewish origin and vice versa. Each could make a reasonable case for being superior, but the end result was a fractured community, with the faultline lying exactly where Paul would wish to see real communion, that is between Jews and Gentiles. Paul's vision of a new non-exclusive people of God, no longer ethnically identifiable, is grounded precisely in his understanding of the cross. As a result, the situation in the Roman communities contradicts a vision which lies at the very heart of Pauline theology. It may be worthwhile to notice how he proceeds.

His marvellous practical advice to the Romans lies in 12:1–15:13, a passage with immense potential today for a pluriform (pluribelle?), re-united Christianity. His advice especially on the *adiaphora*, those elements of faith which are not Church dividing, could be developed in the light of Vatican II's 'hierarchy of doctrines'. Paul could, in theory and in principle, have written this quite practical and inspiring advice to the Romans and left it at that. The letter would then have been a mere four chapters long, instead of the sixteen we have today. In any case, the sixteen chapters seem lenghty in light of the presenting occasion for the letter: looking for a bed for the night en route to Spain! So why the dense and intricate arguments of this letter?

Paul presents his argument in four interlocked, organically articulated moments. In the first moment, chapters 1–4, he states that neither Jew nor Gentile can claim superiority in moral achievement. Both Jew and Greek alike are in need of forgiveness. In the second moment, chapters 5–8, he shows that there is no distinction between Jew and Greek in terms of God's gracious gifts. On both, God has lavished salvation, faith, baptism etc. In the third moment, Paul goes into the difficult area of the role of the chosen people in salvation history, their relationship with the Gentiles and their continued significance in God's eyes. The Jew and the Greek are intricately bound together in God's plan. Paul argues all of these points, powerfully, deeply, incisively, cumulatively. Only then does Paul give his practical advice. Paul *honours* his readers by inviting them to partake in a deep consideration of *why* they should be reconciled before he tells them *how*. He trusts his readers with strong ideas. As a result, the reader/listener knows and is enabled to grasp the motives behind the practical advice before coming to it. In this way, he respects the intelligence of the Romans and honours their own integrity by inviting intellectual engagement of a high, even very high, level. He hopes to be heard, but not blindly obeyed. Again, we can draw conclusions from this for Church leadership today.

LETTERS TO THE CORINTHIANS

My final example comes from the Corinthian correspondence. The relationship with the Corinthians was lively and difficult. The difficulties cannot be laid at one door: the people themselves set too much store by the flashy spiritual gifts and by fine preaching; Paul felt his paternity to be unique and could be 'proprietorial'; the 'opponents' in the community offered a different vision. The upshot was a symbiotic relationship, at one and the same time genuine, lively and in constant need of repair! Of course, we have only one side of the correspondence, but Paul's own words in 2 Corinthians, after yet another attempt at reconciliation, are worthy of note:

> We have spoken frankly to you Corinthians; our heart is wide open to you. There is no restriction in our affections, but only in yours. In return – I speak as to children – open wide your hearts also. (2 Cor 6:11-13)

> Make room in your hearts for us. (2 Cor 7:2)

Perhaps here the parallel with today doesn't quite work, because Paul has not darkened the relationship with any gross failure in stewardship. Nevertheless, in any living relationship the need for reconciliation and forgiveness will always be present and sometimes the forgiveness needed will not be from the top down. The children sometimes have to facilitate the parent towards reconciliation.

AND TODAY?

I noted earlier that we may distinguish the Pauline and the Deutero-Pauline letters. In this respect an interesting datum emerges. In the genuine Pauline letters, the most common metaphor for the assembly of Christians is the *body*. In the Deutero-Pauline letters (1 and 2 Timothy, Titus and most likely Ephesians and Colossians), the main metaphor is that of the *household*. The shift is instructive. It would be commonly conceded that the later letters are evidence of a loss of original courage *vis-à-vis* challenging the dominant culture. The re-assertion of culturally established roles contrasts with the table fellowship of Jesus and Paul's own express obliteration of socially constructed and gendered distinctions. These later documents are also scripture, but we see in them a conforming attitude and a settling-down, a domestication of the revolutionary message of the Gospel. It is not accidental, therefore, that the later documents prefer the hierarchical model of the household, while the genuine Pauline texts prefer the more egalitarian model of the human body. In the image of a body, there is a head, but all the other members of this body need each other.

From this preliminary overview of some Pauline strategies, I think we can see parallels and pointers for today. When Paul speaks, it is noticeable that he has listened carefully to the questions and more importantly to the experience of his hearers. He is sensitive to any falling-off in mutual affection and esteem and carefully responds accordingly. Paul, as well as listening, expects to be listened to. But notice that he really tries to explain the rationale behind any particular advice or teaching. He hopes his counsel will be taken up because it has been understood, not because it has been said. In this regard, his distinction between 'word of the Lord' and 'my own opinion' could be revived in the leadership of the Church. Porous infallibility and false authority are foreign to his mode of teaching. As he persuades by his best argument, and as he gives the grounds for any advice or teaching, he honours not only the intelligence of his hearers but also their integrity and authenticity. It might be good if in Church teaching a greater courage in the reasonableness of faith, both in doctrine and in morals, were evident. Finally, while Paul uses the language of the body for the family of the faith, there are distinctions of roles, from the very start, with a consequent need for reconciliation. Genuine openness, even fragility, is the *sine qua non* of any future reconciliation between the failed leadership of the Church and the dispersed flock. We do all belong to the one body and when one part is sick, we are all sick.

WHERE WE ARE ON OUR OWN

As noted earlier, I do not think our ancient sources can help us directly to read and address our world. The scriptures *can* invite us to do that, just as, for example, Paul is well able to use a variety of cultural codes to put the Gospel across in his time. As the reader will have noticed, he uses religious, philosophical and political codes to read his own culture and re-present the Good News. The philosophical is perhaps especially interesting: Paul is able to use the language of Cynlcism and Stoicism, truly popular philosophies, and able to put them at the service of his proclamation. From Paul's reading of *his* culture, we are indirectly encouraged to read our own, so enormously different from his and even from our own earlier Irish context. What do we see?

Increasingly, we live in a multicultural society, where knowledge and information are the motors driving development and change. The sheer variety and availability of different ideas, beliefs and values have diminished if not erased community consent and conformity. Awareness of the impossible panorama of world views can paralyse and prevent a faith option. For the institutional Church specifically, the loss of standing has strengthened a process of declericalisation and secularisation of convictions. For those 'hanging in', it is difficult to maintain identity in the supermarket of beliefs, where the culture promotes 'believing without belonging'. The new religious movements, those outside ecclesial reference, do continue to acknowledge the hunger for something more, the disillusionment with mere well-being and the fear of anonymity in a globalised econony and society. We cannot see what the future will bring, but emerging Catholicism is showing the following features:

- Catholicism is becoming de-institutionalised, invisible in the culture, with a corresponding new doctrinal flexibility, at a popular level.
- In some quarters, the main reaction of some groups is to become insular, in small groups, with a dogmatic tendency toward *intégrisme*.
- A diffuse and eclectic mysticism, under the general banner of new-age esotericism is detectable.
- There are many symptoms of a re-engagement with 'spirituality' or secular religiosity, expressing and meeting needs not recognised, apparently, by agents of the Church.

As part of this brave new world, at least four considerations are placed before those who would proclaim the Gospel today. First, we won't 'buy into' ideas and teachings that we do not understand. People no longer accept truth on the basis of authoritative proclamation alone: we expect convincing arguments. We also expect an awareness that modes of presentation – models or paradigms – are always limited. Authority is earned, not presumed, something we also find in the gospels ('They were astounded at his teaching, for he taught them as one having authority, and not as the scribes [Mk 1:22]). Second, we expect our experience and opinion to be listened to. The weakening of hierarchical models in others areas of life leads us to expect a fundamental equality of respect and treatment. A leadership which does not listen will not be listened to. Third, as a kind of corollary to the second point, faith flourishes only where there is a sense of tangible belonging, both in terms of communion and in terms of justice. Faith for private consolation with no discernable consequences is unsustainable. As the title of a book put it, a Church which does not serve serves for nothing. Today faith can be sustained only by belonging to some kind of group where I feel myself received and respected, called and challenged. Fourth, my own spiritual journey ought to be very much part of that access to faith. I call these elements the four legs of the table of the faith. If we wish to sit at this table and if this table is to be stable and a real place of hospitality for the whole person, then all four dimensions need to be addressed by the Church: spirituality, understanding, belonging and action. When any two legs no longer function, the table is unstable. The challenge today cannot be met by quick-fix programmes, but rather attending to the whole person, living as we do in the quicksands of post-modernity. We won't know what people need if we do not listen. We won't have bearers of the message into the future if they are not listened to. The obligation to attend to all the dimensions of faith together is one of the gifts wrapped in the challenge of post-modernism.

By way of conclusion, familiarity with the first and perhaps greatest pastor in the New Testament can help us today. Perhaps even independently of Paul as pastor, teacher and reconciler, we might catch his vision and energy, making them our own at the service of the Gospel in our time. Nevertheless, we do live at a peculiar time and we will not find all the resources for the future in the distant past. On the contrary, unless we have the courage to do something really new, then we will not be faithful to the past. To repeat is to falsify. New wine, new wineskins!

Chapter 4

WHY DID PAUL PERSECUTE CHRISTIANS?

In our world, where people are often persecuted for their faith and intra-religious conflict occurs, the question of why Paul persecuted Christians might seem superfluous. After all, intolerance is often the fruit of pious zeal. However, we need to take an imaginative step backwards in time to the religious and cultural context and recent history. Judaism did not persecute other religious bodies. Indeed, Judaism did not even proselytise, as a general rule (an exception will be noted below). The fact that Jews in general did not proselytise – never mind persecute – makes Paul's action against the Christian movement seem out of character for the faith.

THE RELIGIOUS AND CULTURAL CONTEXT

The broad religious and cultural setting is that of the Roman Empire in the first century of our era. Religion was important, very important, in that world. We may notice, however, that that world of many gods and goddesses was inherently tolerant and open. Persecution precisely for your beliefs was, in effect, unknown (with the outstanding exception of Antiochus IV Epiphanes, noted below). When new religious systems were encountered, the tendency was to absorb them, using models from and similarities with the original pantheon. Alternatively, some more deities could simply be added to the mix. Thus, while Jupiter became Zeus and Venus became Aphrodite, Isis was an addition. At the same time, there was a sensitivity regarding public rites and emperor worship. These were regarded as the duty of all citizens. Jews, however, had negotiated a special status for themselves and were not obliged to take part in pagan rites and sacrifices, only to *pray* for the emperor at their own worship. The modern distinction between Church and State was not part of the world view of antiquity. Nevertheless, there were 'wars of religion', even if the issues were viewed differently from each side. We do know, for example, that the Romans *twice* put down serious Jewish revolts, once in AD 70 and then again in AD 135. From a Jewish point of view, the core issue was indeed religion. From the Roman point of view, the core issue was politics and the effective management of the empire. But even if the Roman Empire had conflicts with Judaism and, later on, with Christianity, Judaism itself was not typically a persecuting faith, then or indeed now.

But before the Roman Empire dominated in the area, there *was* an experience of precisely *religious* persecution. In the time of Antiochus IV Epiphanes, a concerted effort was made to eliminate Judaism. This is reflected in the books of Daniel and 1 and 2 Maccabees. Familiar as we are with centuries of persecution of the Jews, the story perhaps causes no surprise. But historians of the period often regard the persecution under Antioch IV as the first instance of religious persecution as such. The story of the mother and her seven sons is a graphic illustration of the issues and the cost to individual lives (2 Macc 7 – with a remarkable echo in 4 Macc 15–18).

> It happened also that seven brothers and their mother were arrested and were being compelled by the king, under torture with whips and thongs, to partake of unlawful swine's flesh. One of them, acting as their spokesman, said, 'What do you intend to ask and learn from us? For we are ready to die rather than transgress the laws of our ancestors'.
>
> The king fell into a rage, and gave orders to have pans and caldrons heated. These were heated immediately, and he commanded that the tongue of their spokesman be cut out and that they scalp him and cut off his hands and feet, while the rest of the brothers and the mother looked on. When he was utterly helpless, the king

ordered them to take him to the fire, still breathing, and to fry him in a pan. The smoke from the pan spread widely, but the brothers and their mother encouraged one another to die nobly, saying, 'The Lord God is watching over us and in truth has compassion on us, as Moses declared in his song that bore witness against the people to their faces, when he said, "And he will have compassion on his servants"'. (2 Macc 7:1-6)

That Judaism itself should persecute anyone else for their faith seems even more remarkable – even unthinkable and in practice impossible, given that they were apparently forbidden to impose the death penalty.

The crisis under Antiochus IV sparked off tremendous upheaval among Jews, a crisis both political and religious, which continued to reverberate in the time of Jesus and Paul. One product of that crisis was the birth of new movements within Judaism, including the movement to which Paul himself belonged, Pharisaism. Pharisees were unusual in that they tried to convert people to the Jewish faith. The harsh words of Jesus in Matthew's gospel capture that aspect: 'Woe to you, scribes and Pharisees, hypocrites! For you cross sea and land to make a single convert, and you make the new convert twice as much a child of hell as yourselves' (Mt 23:15). Of this group of committed believers, Saul the zealous and committed Pharisee was a member.

Within living memory, or at least within recent literary record, Jews had been persecuted for being Jews. This in itself was unusual at the time. Broadly speaking as we saw, religions in antiquity were porous and tolerant. The Jews, however, were careful to keep themselves apart, so much so that they did not even seek converts, with the notable exception of the Pharisees. That Saul, a Pharisee, should have persecuted Christians, from Jewish and Gentile backgrounds, is wholly unusual. And yet he did, as he confesses himself several times and as were read in the Acts of the Apostles:

If anyone else has reason to be confident in the flesh, I have more: circumcised on the eighth day, a member of the people of Israel, of the tribe of Benjamin, a Hebrew born of Hebrews; as to the law, a Pharisee; as to zeal, a persecutor of the Church; as to righteousness under the law, blameless. (Phil 3:4-6)

The Acts of the Apostles mentions Saul as persecutor in chapters 7 and 8, where he is suddenly introduced as 'attending' the stoning of Stephen and then shown actively engaging in searching out and identifying Christians (Acts 8:1-3) with authority from the high priest in Jerusalem (Acts 9:1-2). Within the story of Saul's conversion, it is noted several times that he was indeed a persecutor (Acts 9:3-19, 22:1-21, 26:2-23). Paul himself mentions his previous role a number of times. This is done to further some argument rather than out of biographical interest. We can see this, for example, in the letter to the Galatians 1:13, where he reminds his hearers of his previous role precisely to underline the tremendous change that occurred. According to Paul in Galatians 1:22, this was recognised at the time. The only other mention of his persecution in his own letters is in 1 Corinthians 15:9, again at the service of an argument about the resurrection of the dead. Paul himself is discrete, mentioning his previous persecution only twice. Is it possible to reconstruct why he became so engaged and enraged?

Why Paul persecuted Christians

In the first place, I think we can take for granted that Paul knew what the Christians were saying about Jesus. In later life, dealing with different communities, he shows that he is quite aware of what the issues are and can be very accurate in naming them and responding to them. He has his contacts, his letter-bearers, and sometimes emissaries from the communities to keep him abreast of the personalities and problems. There is no reason to think that the earlier Saul approached things differently. An intelligent, energetic man like St Paul would never have wasted his time opposing something he hadn't understood or about which he hadn't been adequately informed. We are not to think of him as having some kind of free-floating anger 'landing' somehow on the Christians. On the contrary, he knows exactly what they are saying: Jesus the crucified is risen (Rom 4:24, 8:11, 34, 10:9; 2 Cor 4:14; Gal 1:1; 1 Thess 1:10); he is Lord (Rom 10:9; 1 Cor 12:3); he is the messiah of God (Rom 1:1, 4, 6-8, 2:16 etc.); and in him God's promises to Israel are fulfilled. These are the first and most basic claims of the Christian proclamation. Sometimes people ask where Paul 'got' all his beliefs. Part of the answer lies in his awareness of what the first followers of Jesus were saying, perhaps gleaned from personal conversations.

In the second place, Paul was also convinced that the Christians were profoundly, utterly mistaken. He knew they were mistaken because of a text in the book of Deuteronomy. This text mentions 'hanging on a tree' and being 'under God's curse'. It reads thus:

> When someone is convicted of a crime punishable by death and is executed, and you hang him on a tree, his corpse must not remain all night upon the tree; you shall bury him that same day, for anyone hung on a tree is under God's curse. You must not defile the land that the Lord your God is giving you for possession. (Deut 21:22-23)

The wide context is that of the covenant, which bestows blessings and curses; the narrow context is capital punishment. The ones who are blessed are 'in the covenant' and the cursed are 'outside the covenant'. The text could hardly be clearer – whoever is crucified is under *God's* curse. For Saul, the reasoning would have been as follows: God's messiah is supposed to bring the end-time blessings to the world; anyone crucified is in receipt of the diametrical opposite of a blessing, that is, a curse; therefore, the crucified Jesus could not possibly be the messiah. For Jewish believers of the time, the words of the Bible, especially the Pentateuch, were literally the words of

God, given directly by God to Moses. So, the Christians were not just wrong in some matters, such as the indiscriminate inclusion of the Gentiles; they are profoundly mistaken in their understanding of God's plans for his world and for human history. It is helpful, of course, that Paul himself in the letter to the Galatians alludes to this passage, allowing us to safely say that he was aware of it:

> Christ redeemed us from the curse of the law by becoming a curse for us – for it is written, 'Cursed is everyone who hangs on a tree' – in order that in Christ Jesus the blessing of Abraham might come to the Gentiles, so that we might receive the promise of the Spirit through faith. (Gal 3:13-14)

The verses from Galatians are in themselves quite difficult to grasp – an attempt will be made later – but for the moment it is sufficient to notice that Saul the Pharisee and Paul the Apostle knew his Bible extremely well and, we may assume, used this text as a primary argument against the truth of the Christian proclamation. *This* man could not possibly be the messiah God intended to bestow the end-time blessings on Israel and the world. The very word of God makes that clear. The zeal of the Pharisee ignited the zeal of the persecutor.

In the third place, there is no need to oppose religious opinions that are *not spreading*. If the Christian movement were just a few religious enthusiasts, in some holy huddle, it wouldn't have been worth opposing and there would have been no need to expend valuable time and energy on it. If Christianity were just for a few, then Saul would not have bothered to oppose it. The option not to oppose a movement 'that is going nowhere' is present in the New Testament:

> But a Pharisee in the council named Gamaliel, a teacher of the law, respected by all the people, stood up and ordered the men to be put outside for a short time. Then he said to them, 'Fellow Israelites, consider carefully what you propose to do to these men. For

some time ago Theudas rose up, claiming to be somebody, and a number of men, about four hundred, joined him; but he was killed, and all who followed him were dispersed and disappeared. After him Judas the Galilean rose up at the time of the census and got people to follow him; he also perished, and all who followed him were scattered. So in the present case, I tell you, keep away from these men and let them alone; because if this plan or this undertaking is of human origin, it will fail; but if it is of God, you will not be able to overthrow them – in that case you may even be found fighting against God!' They were convinced by him, and when they had called in the apostles, they had them flogged. Then they ordered them not to speak in the name of Jesus, and let them go. (Acts 5:34-41)

Such discerning, faithful tolerance comes from the same Gamaliel who was Paul's teacher: 'I am a Jew, born in Tarsus in Cilicia, but brought up in this city at the feet of Gamaliel, educated strictly according to our ancestral law, being zealous for God, just as all of you are today' (Acts 22:3).

But in the case of the followers of the Nazarene, Paul does not follow the advice of his revered mentor. Christianity is dangerous not just because it is profoundly wrong; it is dangerous because it is leading very many astray. Too much was at stake to leave it alone and to just wait and see how it would evolve. The Christian proclamation was to be opposed precisely because it was gaining adherents, perhaps those very adherents any committed Pharisee would have liked to have netted for his movement.

In the fourth place, we could permit ourselves to surmise that Saul himself sensed the attraction of the Christian proclamation. In other words, he not only understood what Christians were saying, but felt himself the draw of the teaching. This is a bigger assumption than the previous three. Can it be supported? As a Hellenised Jew from the Diaspora, Saul would have been familiar with Gentiles who attached themselves to synagogues, drawn to pure monotheism and the high ethical teaching of Judaism, but who did not 'become Jews', that is, undergo circumcision, but stayed, so to speak, on the edge. These 'devout persons' (Acts 13:43, 50, 16:14, 17:4, 17, 18:7) or 'God fearers' (Acts 10:2, 22, 35, 13:16, 26) could easily have been the first targets of the proselytising missions of the Pharisees. It would, of course, have been easier for them to enter fully into the Christian movement, there being no requirement of circumcision or indeed no need to undertake the socially awkward dietary laws of Judaism. I suspect that the Christian success with the very audience tailor-made for conversion to Judaism would have spurred Saul the Pharisee to deal with the heresy once and for all. Conversely, given that Pharisees liked to make converts, the easier inclusion of outsiders in Christianity may have been part of his own 'appreciation' of what the Christians were up to. They were doing something he would very much like to have been able to do. It may even be that in resisting the Christian Gospel, he was resisting that part of himself which was perhaps perversely drawn to it. It may well be in error to think of his 'conversion' as sudden – very few conversions, when examined closely, are really sudden.

In summary, Saul's persecution of Christians was very unusual for the time and quite exceptional for Jews. Jews have always enjoyed (in both senses) robust arguments and contrasts of opinions. It is really not part of their tradition to *prevent* especially by persecution other Jews from thinking differently. The suggestion here is that Paul's persecution of Jesus' followers is best grasped in the light of the fourfold analysis just offered: he knew the Christian message perfectly well; he was convinced it was utterly mistaken; he saw that it was spreading; and he could see, perhaps even feel, its attraction. Without some such assumptions, it is difficult to fathom why someone of his intelligence, energy and personal charisma would have engaged so fully in a task so apparently at variance with Jewish practice. As it was, the younger Saul acted like the later Paul: he gave it everything he had.

In the light of these assumptions, his 'conversion' was of a most particular kind. It meant for him nothing less than a turning upside down of his personal and religious worlds, while at the same time remaining a Jew. We can see this in a document that may very well be the last from Paul that has come down to us:

> Yet whatever gains I had, these I have come to regard as loss because of Christ. More than that, I regard everything as loss because of the surpassing value of knowing Christ Jesus my Lord. For his sake I have suffered the loss of all things, and I regard them as rubbish, in order that I may gain Christ and be found in him, not having a righteousness of my own that comes from the law, but one that comes through faith in Christ, the righteousness from God based on faith. I want to know Christ and the power of his resurrection and the sharing of his sufferings by becoming like him in his death, if somehow I may attain the resurrection from the dead. (Phil 3:7-11)

Given his previous clear rejection of the crucified Jesus on the firm ground of God's word in Deuteronomy, the 'turning' of Paul was in truth a kind of revolution, first of all for him personally and, because of his ministry, for the shape of Christianity to come. It would take some time for the consequences to register. To this momentous event we now turn.

Chapter 5

THE CONVERSION OF ST PAUL

We are fascinated by stories, real or fictional, in which some extraordinary reversal of fortune or life is recounted. One story of encounter and transformation has had an incalculable effect on the Christian movement: that of Saul of Tarsus, who became the great apostle Paul. What was the nature of his conversion and can it help us today?

Recently a film was released bearing the title of a well-known hymn: 'Amazing Grace'. That hymn was written by John Newton, a slave trader, who experienced a conversion and turned against his previous way of life. In the light of that the words are very moving: 'I once was lost, but now am found, was blind, but now I see.' Sudden and drastic moral change seems to be characteristic of the classical conversion story, and we are reminded of some other great figures of conversion in Christian history: St Augustine, Martin Luther and Cardinal John Henry Newman.

Augustine's conversion was motored by his search for a meaningful understanding of life. In his own words, his heart was restless. We would express it somewhat differently today: Augustine was under considerable existential, psychological, spiritual and emotional stress until he rediscovered for himself Catholic Christianity. From a psychological point of view, Augustine exhibited some symptoms of a nervous breakdown when conversion finally broke.

Martin Luther's conversion came about because of his extraordinarily sensitive conscience and his quest for some absolute reassurance *vis-à-vis* God and salvation. He was tremendously anxious – scrupulous we would say – about 'being saved'. None of the practices of the late medieval Catholic Church brought peace of mind. He found rest in faith and grace alone. This happened, not coincidentally, after he discovered Paul, through the lens of St Augustine. (We may add here that the pre-Christian Paul was not like Luther and showed no evidence of a scrupulous conscience. On the contrary, he seemed perfectly content as a Pharisee and enjoyed a robust attitude to life.)

When John Henry Newman finally left the Church of England for the Catholic Church, the conversion was as much a matter of intellectual conviction as anything else. There was of course, as is the case with Augustine and Martin Luther, a deep emotional dimension to his quest. Perhaps of all three, Newman most resembles Paul: he had objections that had to be overcome.

These are great and genuine conversions motivated by a variety of issues (morality, meaning, conscience, logic) but the change that took place in Saul of Tarsus was actually like none of these. Paul, while still a Pharisee, lived an ethically flawless life. He was not racked by awareness of his own sin. Romans 7 is only a partial guide here because the 'I' is greater than one individual. Neither was he searching for another meaning in life, as if he needed to slake some as yet unidentified thirst for meaning. Paul had all that and more as a faithful and practising Jew.

THE CASE OF ST PAUL

All this makes it harder to understand his conversion unless we ask ourselves two questions: why did he oppose the Christian way so virulently, and what happened to change his mind. While still a Jew, as we just saw, Paul knew Christianity quite well, his sensibilities ensuring that he not go to too much trouble over something he didn't understand. For him, the Christian movement was dangerous – drawing people away from God into an absurd and contradictory religion. And it would not have been at all dangerous if it were not attractive and growing in popularity. There is no need to oppose a movement that is going nowhere. So Paul knew Christian teachings, he thought the movement was dangerous and he was able to appreciate its attractiveness. As we saw in Chapter 4, his opinion that the movement was dangerous came from a text in the Old Testament, the book of Deuteronomy, where we read: 'When someone is convicted of a crime punishable by death and is executed, and you hang him on a tree, his corpse must not remain all night upon the tree; you shall bury him that same day, for anyone hung on a tree is under God's curse. You must not defile the land that the Lord your God is giving you for possession' (Deut 21:22-23). 'Curse' here means the exact opposite of blessing: it means being outside the covenant, outside God's grace. It is a tough text. Paul can be quite logical: if that is in the Bible and the Bible is God's word, then the crucified Jesus cannot be the messiah, because the messiah is supposed to bring blessings, not curses. As so, in horror at a faith so absurd that it contradicts the Bible, Paul used his considerable energies to bring it down.

It is worth remembering again that Paul was not really like John Newton or Martin Luther or even St Augustine: he was not racked by morality or conscience or meaning. He must have felt the attractiveness of Christianity, yet it had to be opposed. What changed him was an encounter with the Risen Lord. Paul never refers to what happened to him as a conversion: he did not use that important early Christian word 'metanoia'. Rather, he talks of his 'turning'. The conversion of Paul is narrated in the New Testament no fewer than four times, that is, three times in the Acts of the Apostles (9:9-19, 22:1-21 and 26:2-23) and once in the letters (Gal 1:11-24). There is a further allusion in 1 Corinthians 15:8, which serves to confirm the essential features as described by Paul himself in Galatians 1. Paul is very cautious in describing this encounter, but here are his own words:

> For I want you to know, brothers and sisters, that the Gospel that was proclaimed by me is not of human origin; for I did not receive it from a human source, nor was I taught it, but I received it through a revelation of

Jesus Christ. You have heard, no doubt, of my earlier life in Judaism. I was violently persecuting the Church of God and was trying to destroy it. I advanced in Judaism beyond many among my people of the same age, for I was far more zealous for the traditions of my ancestors. But when God, who had set me apart before I was born and called me through his grace, was pleased to reveal his Son to me, so that I might proclaim him among the Gentiles, I did not confer with any human being, nor did I go up to Jerusalem to those who were already apostles before me, but I went away at once into Arabia, and afterwards I returned to Damascus. Then after three years I did go up to Jerusalem to visit Cephas and stayed with him fifteen days. (Gal 1:11-18)

In other words, this was a revolution in his world view and it took him a long time to absorb it and come to terms with the consequences. Previously based on scripture, he knew Jesus could not possibly be the messiah, and now based on immediate experience, which he could not deny, he knew Jesus absolutely was alive and risen, messiah and Lord. In a way, his life stopped. He had to re-think his entire religious world and he had to decide on his role within it. We don't know how the Jews felt, but the Christians were amazed at and mistrusted the change. However, despite its distrust, it gained one of the great minds of the first century, who worked for another thirty-five years promoting the Gospel, founding churches and writing letters that continue to challenge and illuminate.

EXPERIENCE BEYOND WORDS

Like all authentic religious experience, this one too was 'beyond words' (to use Paul's own expression about another mystical experience recounted in 2 Corinthians 12). Accounts of deep religious experience are always couched in some kind of symbolic language. In Paul's case the language combines the language of prophetic call (cf. Jer 1:4-5) with the language of Apocalyptic (reveal, revelation). The content of the revelation was the person of Jesus Christ. A later expression lets us into something of the deeply personal dimension of this when Paul writes, again in Galatians: 'And the life I now live in the flesh I live by faith in the Son of God, who loved me and gave himself for me' (2:20).

The encounter with Christ made it absolutely clear that this Jesus was raised from the dead, but that conviction came not simply as 'information' but in the form of being loved and a new conviction about the death of Jesus because 'he gave himself for me'. Paul, who previously knew from God's word that the Christian proclamation was false, now had to ask himself a difficult question. Paul had to bring together his earlier biblical conviction and his new realisation that Jesus was raised and therefore was the messiah of God. If whoever hangs on a tree is a curse, that is, 'outside' the covenant blessings, what is God's messiah doing in that place of curse? As a faithful Pharisee, Paul could give only one answer: God's messiah is there because that is precisely where God *wants him to be*. The messiah of God stands with those outside the covenant to bring in those outside, in a gesture of profound identification and solidarity.

The multi-layered experience of encountering the risen Christ entailed a series of movements in Paul's religious imagination. He now *knew* Jesus was the messiah, bringing God's presence among the excluded. This encounter with the risen Lord constitutes Paul's conversion. Paul's own 'conversion' then entailed in itself his calling as an apostle. As a deeply committed person of faith, his desire was to do the will of God. Now that he saw God's will revealed in Jesus, he himself could not but be engaged in this final instalment of God's project. It may be worth underlining once more that Paul did not see himself as 'changing his religion' and in a very real sense he was and remained a Jew. He claims this identity several times in his letters. Nevertheless, he knew also that most of his fellow Jews did not make the step of faith Paul himself made, and it caused him deep pain.

What happened next? Before we come to the Paul of the letters, the Paul we know today, we need to remember that before the journeys began, Paul spent the next fifteen or sixteen years proclaiming the Gospel in Syria and Cilicia, his own home territory. Even before that, there were the three years in Damascus, including the time in Arabia. It is reasonable to surmise that much of the earlier period was spent reconstructing his view of his world, his God and himself.

Chapter 6

THE CROSS IN PAUL'S VISION OF FAITH[1]

It is often said that the Church of the Holy Sepulchre in Jerusalem disappoints visitors. So much is this the case that an alternative 'venue' has been declared, the so-called Garden Tomb. However, it would seem that the Church really does commemorate the spot where Jesus' body was laid. Given the prominence of the resurrection *edicule* in the church itself, it is easy to ignore the other significant shrine, that of the crucifixion. Perhaps the excess of devotional art and the legendary association with the grave of Adam tend to diminish its importance. Nevertheless, somewhere in this area, perhaps on this outcrop of earth, the crucifixion took place. For a modern visitor to the Old City, it can be hard to keep in mind that Jesus' execution took place *outside* the city boundaries. Yet, as we know, this was the case. This status of 'outsider' can stand metaphorically for Paul's understanding of the cross, in a way that is potentially illuminating today. I emphasise *today*, because I believe that we Christians are in need of a new model of redemption. The classical western model has substantially collapsed, in my opinion, and it has not been replaced by another, equally all-embracing theory of redemption.

OUR TRADITIONAL UNDERSTANDING

A convenient contemporary place to evoke the old model of redemption might be Mel Gibson's film, *The Passion of the Christ.*

---

1 An earlier version of this chapter originally appeared in Bible et Terre Sainte, (José Enrique Aguilar Chiu, Kieran J. O'Mahony and Maurice Roger, eds), Peter Lang Publishing, 2008.

While using all the techniques of modern film-making, it seemed to me an old-fashioned project, in its concentration on the suffering and wounds of Jesus. Attention to such details emerged in the Middle Ages and the reticence, silence even, of the gospels is, in contrast, noticeable. That said, I think it does reflect a view of Jesus' death that dominated for the best part of a thousand years. Traditionally – I certainly received it as a child – Jesus' death on the cross was presented exclusively as a punishment for the sins of humanity. More fully expressed, we had a large story arc, which brought together the Fall of Adam (treated as historical fact), original sin, the honour of God who was offended, coupled with the realisation that no human being could 'undo' the offence – only a human who was also divine could undo the offence. It was a kind of religious 'theory of everything': it described the human condition and the need for redemption; it accounted for the suffering of Jesus and laid the ground for the existence of the Church and the sacraments of baptism and confession; it even explained why we feel guilt and remorse, why we die and what we may hope for. Thus, the theory touched human history as a whole, the Christian story in particular, reaching into the deep existential experience of the individual. It was immensely successful in all the churches of the west – not only in the Catholic Church, but also in the churches of the Reform.

There are several problems with this model, of which I shall briefly mention four. First, as expounded classically by Anselm of Canterbury, this model is embedded in the language and cultural presuppositions of feudalism. The honour relations of lord and serf lie behind the understanding of the offence of Adam's sin, as does the impotence of the lower offending party. Second, this model, at least as commonly received, is unable to integrate the resurrection into the salvation event. As is well known, traditionally redemption had been accomplished on the cross (the paying of the price) and the resurrection became an adjunct, the greatest miracle, the proof of divinity. Whether anyone has ever been persuaded by this 'proof' is a moot point. Third, can the sin of Adam be taken as history, as a real event, today? Or does Genesis describe the human condition rather than explain it? The Anselmian model depends on the historicity of Adam's sin. If there is no *historical* sin as such, then the model is itself mortally wounded. And fourth, does that God exist, who is so angry and so offended that he must have satisfaction, the price of sin paid by the terrible suffering of Jesus? Much has been made in the churches of the west of the details of this suffering but, in spite of its venerability, this tradition is more Mel Gibson than Gospel; the gospels themselves are notably reticent.

The collapse of this 'theory of everything' has left western Christians in the lurch. Not only must we try to show that there is a God; not only must we deal with the reality and goodness of other religions; but also at this critical time in Christian religious history, we are without a genuinely popular theology of salvation, which talks our language and speaks to the concerns of our times. The lack of a shared understanding of the events of salvation is a tremendous shortcoming, perhaps more felt than observed. The old has gone but the new has not arrived. We need to go back to our biblical resources; St Paul, especially, has a perspective on this which can be difficult to grasp at first, but which is full of potential for today.

The appropriate place to begin is the conversion of St Paul. As we just saw, Paul knew Christian teachings, he considered the movement dangerous and he was able to appreciate its attractiveness. Perhaps his Pharisaic background also made him sensitive to the missionary dimension of early Christianity. His *theological* opinion that the movement was positively dangerous came from a text in the Old Testament, the book of Deuteronomy, as we saw:

> When someone is convicted of a crime punishable by death and is executed, and you hang him on a tree, his corpse must not remain all night upon the tree; you shall bury him that same day, for anyone hung on a tree

is under God's curse. You must not defile the land that the Lord your God is giving you for possession. (Deut 21:22-23)

WITH A CRUCIFIED MESSIAH

As a consistently logical mind, Paul had to ask himself the next obvious question: why was God's messiah hanging on a tree, becoming a curse, joining the alienated? And, as was already discussed, as a man of deep faith, he concluded that this happened because of God's providence and because this is where God wanted his messiah to be. But why? Because this astonishing solidarity with those excluded from the blessings marked a new moment in God's dealings with humanity: from now on the distinctions Jew and Gentile, insider and outsider, heir of the covenant and alien from the blessings would be no more. The key text here is Galatians:

> Christ redeemed us from the curse of the law by becoming a curse for us – for it is written: 'Cursed is everyone who hangs on a tree' – in order that in Christ Jesus the blessing of Abraham might come to the Gentiles, so that we might receive the promise of the Spirit through faith. (Gal 3:13-14)

The clue here is the bringing together of the Deuteronomic text with the opening of salvation to the Gentiles. Because he knew from immediate experience that Jesus was in fact the messiah, God's messiah on the cross, that is, in a place of curse, outside the blessing, Paul now knew that God's desire was to bring in those previously 'outside'. To use a contemporary term, the cross represented God's solidarity, in Christ, with the excluded, so that those outside the blessing might be brought in. This may seem to us an unusual way to speak of Christ's death. In the past, of course, this text was taken to cohere with punishment theories of redemption – the curse was God's punishing Jesus for our sins. But that is anachronistic. A contextual reading would suggest not punishment but solidarity. This is expressed perfectly in the letter to the Ephesians:

> For he is our peace; in his flesh he has made both groups into one and has broken down the dividing wall, that is, the hostility between us. He has abolished the law with its commandments and ordinances, that he might create in himself one new humanity in place of the two, thus making peace, and might reconcile both groups to God in one body through the cross, thus putting to death that hostility through it. (Eph 2:14-16)

What did Paul think Jesus was 'doing' for us on the cross? Again, a text from Galatians is our clue:

> We ourselves are Jews by birth and not Gentile sinners; yet we know that a person is justified not by the works of the law but through *the* faith *of* Jesus Christ. And we have come to *have faith* in Christ Jesus, so that we might be justified by *the* faith *of* Christ, and not by doing the works of the law, because no one will be justified by the works of the law. But if, in our effort to be justified in Christ, we ourselves have been found to be sinners, is Christ then a servant of sin? Certainly not! But if I build up again the very things that I once tore down, then I demonstrate that I am a transgressor. For through the law I died to the law, so that I might live to God. I have been crucified with Christ; and it is no longer I who live, but it is Christ who lives in me. And the life I now live in the flesh I live by *the* faith *of* the Son of God, who loved me and gave himself for me. I do not nullify the grace of God; for if justification comes through the law, then Christ died for nothing. (Gal 2:15-21; emphasis added)

On the cross, Jesus trusted in God. His identification with the excluded is a measure of the love of God for all, without discrimination. This was felt personally by Paul, as we see in the words 'who loved me' and 'gave himself for me'. As a consequence, our relationship with God builds on that faith, which Jesus himself had as he faced death. We do indeed come to God by faith, as the Reformers said – that is, our faith in the faith which Jesus himself had. If this is right, then the death of Jesus on the cross is not a *sacrifice up* to God to appease his anger and give him the satisfaction he requires, but on the contrary a most compassionate *gesture down* from God, reaching deeply into the heart of every human being.

The writer of the letter to the Hebrews appreciated this teaching fully and profoundly, when he/she wrote:

> Since, therefore, the children share flesh and blood, he himself likewise shared the same things, so that through death he might destroy the one who has the power of death, that is, the devil, and free those who all their lives were held in slavery by the fear of death. For it is clear that he did not come to help angels, but the descendants of Abraham. Therefore he had to become like his brothers and sisters in every respect, so that he might be a merciful and faithful high priest in the service of God, to make a sacrifice of atonement for the sins of the people. Because he himself was tested by what he suffered, he is able to help those who are being tested. (Heb 2:14-18)

Even if the language of atonement appears here, it is modified by the core theology of solidarity. A very priestly understanding of the death of Jesus encounters the following challenges: first, the historical Jesus was not a priest; second, his death was outside a sacred space, and even outside the precincts of the Holy City; third, human blood is the most ritually impure bodily fluid; fourth, according to Deuteronomy, as we have seen, crucifixion was a curse, not a blessing.

A priestly understanding can be achieved, as we see from the Letter to the Hebrews, the New Testament Apocalypse and, perhaps, chapter seventeen of the fourth Gospel, but only by so reconsidering sacrifice that it loses its chief traditional meaning of appeasement or satisfaction.

Finally, this reading of the death of Jesus has a considerable advantage in that it makes the death of Jesus cohere with his ministry. The ministry of Jesus, which was especially towards the excluded, and his proclamation of the indiscriminate love of God and his death are really one event: God's love for all without distinction, loving us even to the point of solidarity with us all in the destruction and ultimately universal alienation of death. It is an astounding and arresting picture of God. It is a deeply encouraging insight into the depths of God's love for all humanity and for us today. Once St Paul saw this he knew immediately what the rest of his life was going to be like: telling people about this, because *this* proclamation, this Good News, cannot be kept to ourselves, once it has dawned on us. St Paul writes very movingly in the second chapter of the letter to the Galatians: 'And the life I now live in the flesh I live by faith in the Son of God, who loved me and gave himself for me' (Gal 2:20). It is the only time he speaks of Jesus the Son of God, *who loved me*.

If this is right, then, as was said above, the death of Jesus on the cross is not a sacrifice up to God to appease his anger and give him the satisfaction he requires, but on the contrary a most compassionate gesture down from God, reaching deeply into the heart of every human being. Each of us is now invited to live by the faith of the Son of God, who loved me and gave himself for me.

To go back to my starting point: Paul's theology of cross, sketched briefly here, can help us build a new theology of salvation for today. First, it takes us away from the feudal world of honour/shame and brings us into a relational model of solidarity. Second, the resurrection is integral to the salvation event, bringing us from solidarity with the excluded to final, eternal justice. Third, an historical sin of Adam is not essential. It is sufficient that the doctrine of original sin should describe the human condition without analysing the causes. Fourth, the God who reaches so deeply and personally into the human condition does not desire satisfaction for insult, but rather love in response to love. Of course, more can and would need to be said; nevertheless, perhaps enough has been said to suggest the potential for renewing our language of salvation today. When we next visit the Church of the Holy Sepulchre, we can recall that once it lay outside the Holy City, but now, quite fittingly, it has been brought in, just as the death of Jesus in this very spot brought in those who were formally outside the dispensation of the covenant.

Chapter 7

WHY IS EASTER AT THE CENTRE?

It is more than appropriate that the reading that first proclaims the resurrection at the Easter Vigil should come from St Paul. He is, after all, the only first-generation Christian to give us a personal account of his experience of the Risen Lord. Naturally, this is of special interest to us, even apart from the fact that Paul is the earliest writer to survive from the first Christian century.

At the same time, when writing of his encounters with the Risen Lord, Paul is markedly cautious, almost unwilling. In Galatians 1, he says, in a very lapidary manner:

> For I want you to know, brothers and sisters, that the Gospel that was proclaimed by me is not of human origin; for I did not receive it from a human source, nor was I taught it, but I received it through a revelation of Jesus Christ ... But when God, who had set me apart before I was born and called me through his grace, was pleased to reveal his Son to me, so that I might proclaim him among the Gentiles, I did not confer with any human being, nor did I go up to Jerusalem to those who were already apostles before me, but I went away at once into Arabia, and afterwards I returned to Damascus. (Gal 1:11-12, 15-17)

All religious language comes from a particular time and place. Paul's language here reflects the call of Jeremiah and the style of Jewish apocalyptic writing. 'Now the word of the Lord came to me saying, "Before I formed you in the womb I knew you, and before you were

born I consecrated you; I appointed you a prophet to the nations'"
(Jer 1:4-5). For the Apocalyptic dimension, reference to the book of
Revelation will suffice to illustrate the spiritual context:

> The revelation of Jesus Christ, which God gave him to
> show his servants what must soon take place; he made
> it known by sending his angel to his servant John, who
> testified to the word of God and to the testimony of
> Jesus Christ, even to all that he saw. (Rev 1:1-2)

PAUL IN HIS OWN FAITH SETTING

Paul, as a Pharisee, was an apocalyptic Jew. 'Apocalyptic' has a
popular meaning which doesn't help us here. In the setting of the turn
of the eras, it really means both a world view and a literary style. In the
world view, those faithful to God are reassured that there is a guiding
hand in history and that a day is coming when God will finally
vindicate those who have been faithful. As a literary style, it usually
entails a complex metaphorical vision, often in the form of a
revelation to a seer. The importance of this world view for Paul can
be seen from the use of the word 'apocalypse' both as verb and as
noun in his authentic writings (Rom 1:17-18, 2:5, 8:18-19, 16:25; 1
Cor 1:7, 2:10, 3:13, 14:6, 26, 30; 2 Cor 12:1, 7; Gal 1:12, 16, 2:2,
3:23; Phil 3:15; 2 Thess 1:7, 2:3, 6, 8). Perhaps the most famous
instance is in 1 Thessalonians:

> Now concerning the times and the seasons, brothers
> and sisters, you do not need to have anything written
> to you. For you yourselves know very well that the day
> of the Lord will come like a thief in the night. When
> they say, 'There is peace and security', then sudden
> destruction will come upon them, as labour pains come
> upon a pregnant woman, and there will be no escape!
> But you, beloved, are not in darkness, for that day to
> surprise you like a thief; for you are all children of light

and children of the day; we are not of the night or of darkness. So then let us not fall asleep as others do, but let us keep awake and be sober; for those who sleep at night, and those who are drunk get drunk at night. But since we belong to the day, let us be sober, and put on the breastplate of faith and love, and for a helmet the hope of salvation. For God has destined us not for wrath but for obtaining salvation through our Lord Jesus Christ, who died for us, so that whether we are awake or asleep we may live with him. Therefore encourage one another and build up each other, as indeed you are doing. (1 Thess 5:1-11)

In this world view, God's act of justice at the end of time will include the resurrection of the dead. Paul, while still a Pharisee, would have believed in the resurrection of the dead.

Listen, I will tell you a mystery! We will not all die, but we will all be changed, in a moment, in the twinkling of an eye, at the last trumpet. For the trumpet will sound, and the dead will be raised imperishable, and we will be changed. (1 Cor 15:51-53)

So when Paul talks in Galatians about his conversion and uses the term 'reveal', a great deal is implied. This wasn't simply a spiritual encounter, it was a revelation of God's purpose in history, anticipated in the resurrection of Jesus, and unveiled to Paul when he 'met' the risen Lord.

In one other place in his letters, he talks about a similar, later experience, but again with great caution:

I know a person in Christ who fourteen years ago was caught up to the third heaven – whether in the body or out of the body I do not know; God knows. And I know that such a person – whether in the body or out of the body I do not know; God knows – was caught up into Paradise and heard things that are not to be told, that no mortal is permitted to repeat. On behalf of such a one I will boast, but on my own behalf I will not boast, except of my weaknesses. (2 Cor 12:2-5)

The embedded denials are notable. Paul is right to be careful when describing such deep experiences simply because such experiences are of their nature beyond words, as he himself says. In fact, in all religious talk we have to use metaphors, images taken from our limited experience, to try to hold on and express experiences for which we have no words. We have to use *our* language for something for which there is *no* language.

RESURRECTION AND RESUSCITATION

As we saw, even before St Paul encountered the Risen Lord, he was already familiar with Christian teaching about Jesus. He was aware that the first generation of Christians believed, as we do, that Christ was triumphant after death, and to express that they used a range of symbolic expressions. For instance, they said Jesus had sat down at the right hand of God. This is clearly a metaphor, as God has no hands! They also said Jesus had ascended – not, of course, literally, a journey up into space, but spiritually, a journey of transcendence into God. They used other expressions too, such as 'exalted' (Phil 2:9) and 'glorified' (very frequent in the fourth Gospel: Jn 7:39, 11:4, 12:16, 23, 28, 13:31-32, 14:13, 15:8, 17:4, 10). But the key theological expression then, as now, was resurrection. Perhaps the earliest formula of proclamation which has come down to us is: 'They were saying, "The Lord has risen indeed, and he has appeared to Simon!"' (Lk 24:34). At the very centre of Paul's new world view stands the resurrection of Jesus. It is the keystone holding up the entire arch of faith.

We may ask, what does resurrection mean? If St Paul were here now, we might like to ask him three questions: How do you *understand* resurrection? How are we supposed to *imagine* that kind of transcendent existence? And not least, how do you *know* all this?

UNDERSTANDING THE RESURRECTION

What did the early Christians mean when they said Christ is risen from the dead? They meant a great deal more than simply he was alive after death. You may be aware that in the Old Testament there is almost no doctrine of life after death. There are some exceptions to this – for instance the ascent of Elijah in the fiery chariot – but largely they believed in God *for this life only*. But among the very last books of the Bible, such a doctrine emerges as *resurrection*. We see this in the book of Daniel and in the second book of Maccabees. There is a metaphorical anticipation of the teaching in Ezekiel 37, but there the word 'resurrection' – in spite of the tremendous physical descriptions – is a metaphor for the rebirth of Israel after the return home from the Babylonian Exile (587–537 BC). However, a real doctrine of life after death in the form of resurrection is apparent in Daniel and 2 Maccabees.

What triggered the emergence of such a conviction? The Old Testament doctrine of retribution has proved inadequate. According to that traditional teaching, God is just and rewards the good *in this life* and punishes the wicked *in this life*. They clung to such conviction in spite of contrary experiences (cf. Psalms 37 and 73) because they trusted in a just God, and given that there was no life after death, then the reward and punishment simply had to happen during one's earthly life.

Daniel and 2 Maccabees were written at a time of religious persecution. These books worried about all the suffering and injustice that people experience, *which are unresolved at death*. The concrete case they had in mind was that of martyrdom. Given that martyrs have been extraordinarily faithful, even to the point of death, when *could* this just God reward them? In order to continue to speak of God as just, they evolved a theology of resurrection, by which they meant God's final justice to all who have been faithful to him. They were not really speculating about the everlasting soul but trying to continue to believe in a just God. Both of these books teach that the creator God, who called us into existence, can hold us in being across the bar of the bodily destruction in death. For these writers, resurrection was not simply survival or resuscitation. For them, resurrection is God's act of justice, hope and love, in which God will make right all the unresolved experience of injustice and suffering in the world.

The key, I think, is that resurrection is a way of talking about a communitarian experience of God's justice and goodness *when history is over*. In so far as it is a future happening outside of history, it is not properly 'historical' but trans-historical. It is worth repeating that it was not existential anxiety about death that led to this teaching. It was, rather, the quest for the justice of God towards those who had been faithful to the point of death, that is, martyrs. For such martyrs, faithful to the point of death, by definition, there is no time within history for God to act justly towards them. As a result, resurrection and the end of history were inextricably bound together.

IMAGINING THE NEXT STAGE

With exceptions such as the Sadducees, many Jews at the time of Jesus believed in such a future resurrection of the dead, at the end of time, when history was over. In particular, Pharisees – and as we know, St Paul was a Pharisee – believed in the final resurrection of the dead. When the first Christians proclaimed Jesus as risen, they were not only saying that he was alive, but also and even more so, that God's loving act of justice for all humanity had been brought forward, anticipated in the resurrection of Jesus. In other words, they didn't think of resurrection as only or even chiefly individual survival of death or personal resuscitation, but as something God was going to do for all humanity, now unexpectedly brought forward in Jesus. That explains why St Paul, along with many others, thought that the end of the world was near. In one sense, they were right: the end had started, and in this way they were reading the metaphor consistently. 'Resurrection' became the dominant metaphor because it combined both the individual and the end of history as such.

DO WE STILL NEED ST PAUL?

In 1 Corinthians 15:35-36, Paul puts a question on the mouth of his hearers: 'But someone will ask, "How are the dead raised? With what kind of body do they come?"' The next word doesn't encourage: 'Fool!' However, Paul relents a little from that and goes on to give a kind of explanation or an attempt to picture how we may imagine what cannot be, literally, imagined. He begins with the imagery of transformation from nature itself, starting with the seed and wheat or some other grain. The relationship between our existence now and our existence in the future is like the relationship between an acorn and an oak. In other words, the next stage of life is utter transformation, which we cannot really picture. With this imagery, Paul is trying to unsettle a univocal understanding of body and at the same time hold together both continuity and transformation, identity and transcendence. A Church of Ireland ordinand put it to me like this: just as the child in the womb cannot image life outside the womb – that inevitable, necessary and wonderful next stage – likewise we, in the womb of the world, cannot grasp the next stage of life with God. So it was also with Jesus in resurrection: 'What no eye has seen, nor ear heard, nor the human heart conceived, what God has prepared for those who love him' (1 Cor 2:9). The very helpful language of womb and maternal gestation belongs to the language of apocalyptic, and we read from Paul himself: 'We know that the whole creation has been groaning in labour pains until now; and not only the creation, but we ourselves, who have the first fruits of the Spirit, groan inwardly while we wait for adoption, the redemption of our bodies' (Rom 8:22-23).

In itself, this is a late echo of the language we saw above in 1 Thessalonians: 'When they say, "There is peace and security," then sudden destruction will come upon them, as labour pains come upon a pregnant woman, and there will be no escape!' (1 Thess 5:3).

HOW DID PAUL KNOW ALL THIS?

Finally, we may ask, how did St Paul *know* all this? He is, as we saw, very guarded, but we can say that his faith in Jesus risen from the dead is grounded first in an irreducible personal experience. While a Pharisee, he already believed God was a God of justice. This God would, at the end of time, make good the injustices, inequalities and suffering of the innocent. This was a faith conviction. And then, he had his experience of the Risen Lord, however that came about. He knew from inexpressible experience that God had acted to bring about this 'making good', in Jesus. Eventually, this personal experience found expression in the creed of the early communities:

> For I handed on to you as of first importance what I in turn had received: that Christ died for our sins in accordance with the scriptures, and that he was buried, and that he was raised on the third day in accordance with the scriptures, and that he appeared to Cephas, then to the twelve. (1 Cor 15:3-5)

Second, St Paul knew from his own continued spiritual experience that the risen Lord was already at work in him, bringing about that transformation of himself which would be completed in his own participation in Jesus' resurrection from the dead. The reading from Romans read at the Easter Vigil is very eloquent:

> For if we have been united with him in a death like his, we will certainly be united with him in a resurrection like his. We know that our old self was crucified with him so that the body of sin might be destroyed, and we might no longer be enslaved to sin. For whoever has died is freed from sin. But if we have died with Christ, we believe that we will also live with him. We know that Christ, being raised from the dead, will never die again; death no longer has dominion over him. The death he died, he died to sin, once for all; but the life he lives, he lives to God. So you also must consider yourselves dead to sin and alive to God in Christ Jesus. (Rom 6:5-11)

DO WE STILL NEED ST PAUL?

In a very personal note, the now already old Paul could still write:

> Yet whatever gains I had, these I have come to regard as loss because of Christ. More than that, I regard everything as loss because of the surpassing value of knowing Christ Jesus my Lord. For his sake I have suffered the loss of all things, and I regard them as rubbish, in order that I may gain Christ and be found in him, not having a righteousness of my own that comes from the law, but one that comes through faith in Christ, the righteousness from God based on faith. I want to know Christ and the power of his resurrection and the sharing of his sufferings by becoming like him in his death, if somehow I may attain the resurrection from the dead. Not that I have already obtained this or have already reached the goal; but I press on to make it my own, because Christ Jesus has made me his own. Beloved, I do not consider that I have made it my own; but this one thing I do: forgetting what lies behind and straining forward to what lies ahead, I press on toward the goal for the prize of the heavenly call of God in Christ Jesus. (Phil 3:7-15)

It is perhaps a little extreme to put it like this, but Paul, the great preacher of faith, at a certain level knew Jesus was risen from the dead.

Our journey of life and faith can bear a resemblance to that of St Paul: encounter and transformation, leading to celebration. We do have our own encounters with the Lord; we are on our own pilgrimage of transformation; as Christians, we have a joy to celebrate. Before our faith encounters and existential transformation, before St Paul's encounter and transformation, there stands what God was doing in Jesus.

For the Son of God, Jesus Christ, whom we proclaimed among you, Silvanus and Timothy and I, was not 'Yes and No'; but in him it is always 'Yes'. For in him every one of God's promises is a 'Yes'. For this reason it is through him that we say the 'Amen', to the glory of God. (2 Cor 1:19-20)

When we say 'yes' to God's astonishing 'yes' in Jesus, then we can make our own the exultant words of St Paul: 'But thanks be to God, who gives us the victory through our Lord Jesus Christ.' (1 Cor 15:57)

Chapter 8

ST PAUL AND SUFFERING

As we know both from experience and from reflection, suffering, especially innocent suffering, is a tremendous challenge to belief in the existence of a God both good and just. The question is already confronted in the Bible – see for example Psalms 37 and 73, and naturally the book of Job. Christian believers are aware that our faith in Jesus as the messiah and Son of God brings a new dimension to the conversation, that is, God's own participation in suffering and even evil. Paul himself, with his particular understanding of the crucifixion, offers us a path through suffering. This is offered indirectly through reflection on his own experience of dealing with suffering in his life. He may provide some illumination for us today.

PAUL'S EXPERIENCE OF SUFFERING

At the very start, it is worth noting that Paul knows suffering from both sides, so to speak. As we saw, he inflicted suffering on the early Christians. In particular, he seems to have assisted – passively in any case – at the stoning of Stephen. And in the course of his ministry, he sometimes inflicts suffering, as he confesses to the Corinthians in a remarkable passage:

> Now I rejoice, not because you were grieved, but because your grief led to repentance; for you felt a godly grief, so that you were not harmed in any way by us. For godly grief produces a repentance that leads to salvation and brings no regret, but worldly grief produces death. For see what earnestness this godly grief has produced in you, what eagerness to clear yourselves, what

indignation, what alarm, what longing, what zeal, what punishment! At every point you have proved yourselves guiltless in the matter. (2 Cor 7:9-11)

As for Paul himself, his own experience of suffering may be outlined in the following stages: suffering for the churches; physical trials; apostolic trials; emotional trials; suffering and his own spiritual journey.

1.   SUFFERING FOR THE CHURCHES

Paul had a long ministry with fellow workers in Antioch. In the Acts of the Apostle 15, there is a report of a break-up between Paul and Barnabas. The latter is mentioned regularly in the Acts (4:36, 9:27, 11:22, 25, 30, 12:25–13:2, 13:7, 42-43, 46, 50, 14:1, 12, 14, 20, 15:2, 12, 22, 25, 35-37, 39) and in the letters of Paul (1 Cor 9:6; Gal 2:1, 9, 13). The mentions in the letters show, perhaps, a trace of bitterness: 'And the other Jews joined him in this hypocrisy, so that even Barnabas was led astray by their hypocrisy' (Gal 2:13).

The break with Barnabas, a long-standing fellow worker, was emotionally difficult:

> After some days Paul said to Barnabas, 'Come, let us return and visit the believers in every city where we proclaimed the word of the Lord and see how they are doing'. Barnabas wanted to take with them John called Mark. But Paul decided not to take with them one who had deserted them in Pamphylia and had not accompanied them in the work. The disagreement became so sharp that they parted company; Barnabas took Mark with him and sailed away to Cyprus. (Acts 15:36-39)

There were other disagreements, such as that with Peter, but they seem to have been resolved to some degree.

In Thessalonica, Paul had followed his normal practice of setting up the community and then moving on. As we saw, he himself had to really *love* the communities he founded – otherwise the Gospel would have been by word only. As a result, an intense relationship grew up between Paul and the Thessalonians. They found it very disconcerting when he moved on, and when he did not return, sending someone else instead of coming himself. Their pain at this treatment also causes Paul considerable pain, as he writes:

> As for us, brothers and sisters, when, for a short time, we were made orphans by being separated from you – in person, not in heart – we longed with great eagerness to see you face to face. For we wanted to come to you – certainly I, Paul, wanted to again and again – but Satan blocked our way. For what is our hope or joy or crown of boasting before our Lord Jesus at his coming? Is it not you? Yes, you are our glory and joy! Therefore when we could bear it no longer, we decided to be left alone in Athens; and we sent Timothy, our brother and co-worker for God in proclaiming the gospel of Christ, to strengthen and encourage you for the sake of your faith, so that no one would be shaken by these persecutions. Indeed, you yourselves know that this is what we are destined for. In fact, when we were with you, we told you beforehand that we were to suffer persecution; so it turned out, as you know. For this reason, when I could bear it no longer, I sent to find out about your faith; I was afraid that somehow the tempter had tempted you and that our labour had been in vain.
> (1 Thess 2:17–3:5)

The language is very revealing. Earlier, and as mentioned in Chapter 3, he has described himself as a wet nurse (feeding her own children, and therefore taking no pay). Now he uses language to show that he feels the pain they feel – he is their 'parent', yet he too feels like an 'orphan' because of the separation.

A tremendous example of Paul's suffering for the churches may be found in the entire letter to the Galatians. He himself is so bewildered by their adoption of circumcision and dietary laws that he can manage no thanksgiving at the start of the letter, but goes straight in:

> I am astonished that you are so quickly deserting the one who called you in the grace of Christ and are turning to a different gospel – not that there is another gospel, but there are some who are confusing you and want to pervert the gospel of Christ. But even if we or an angel from heaven should proclaim to you a gospel contrary to what we proclaimed to you, let that one be accursed! As we have said before, so now I repeat, if anyone proclaims to you a gospel contrary to what you received, let that one be accursed! (Gal 1:6-9)

Anger comes out clearly in the theology and in the rhetoric of the letter:

> Listen! I, Paul, am telling you that if you let yourselves be circumcised, Christ will be of no benefit to you. Once again I testify to every man who lets himself be circumcised that he is obliged to obey the entire law. You who want to be justified by the law have cut yourselves off from Christ; you have fallen away from grace. For through the Spirit, by faith, we eagerly wait for the hope of righteousness. For in Christ Jesus neither circumcision nor uncircumcision counts for anything; the only thing that counts is faith working through love. (Gal 5:2-6)

But my friends, why am I still being persecuted if I am still preaching circumcision? In that case the offence of the cross has been removed. I wish those who unsettle you would castrate themselves! (Gal 5:11-12)

The measure of his own pain is caught in the birthing imagery to which he returns in chapter 4:

Friends, I beg you, become as I am, for I also have become as you are. You have done me no wrong. You know that it was because of a physical infirmity that I first announced the gospel to you; though my condition put you to the test, you did not scorn or despise me, but welcomed me as an angel of God, as Christ Jesus. What has become of the good will you felt? For I testify that, had it been possible, you would have torn out your eyes and given them to me. Have I now become your enemy by telling you the truth? They make much of you, but for no good purpose; they want to exclude you, so that you may make much of them. It is good to be made much of for a good purpose at all times, and not only when I am present with you. My little children, for whom I am again in the pain of childbirth until Christ is formed in you, I wish I were present with you now and could change my tone, for I am perplexed about you. (Gal 4:12-20)

Perhaps of all the communities, the Corinthian community offered the greatest challenge to Paul. The first four chapters of the first letter are given over to 'sorting' out Paul's relationship with the Corinthians as their father in the faith (1 Cor 4:15). This travail, however, is as nothing compared to the breakdown of relationships which caused the substance of 2 Corinthians 1–7. Paul spells out his very own ministry as precisely that of reconciliation – hence his own intense suffering when he is part of a collapse:

> From now on, therefore, we regard no one from a human point of view; even though we once knew Christ from a human point of view, we know him no longer in that way. So if anyone is in Christ, there is a new creation: everything old has passed away; see, everything has become new! All this is from God, who reconciled us to himself through Christ, and has given us the ministry of reconciliation; that is, in Christ God was reconciling the world to himself, not counting their trespasses against them, and entrusting the message of reconciliation to us. So we are ambassadors for Christ, since God is making his appeal through us; we entreat you on behalf of Christ, be reconciled to God. For our sake he made him to be sin who knew no sin, so that in him we might become the righteousness of God. (2 Cor 5:16-21)

His appeal to them could hardly be more emotional:

> We have spoken frankly to you Corinthians; our heart is wide open to you. There is no restriction in our affections, but only in yours. Make room in your hearts for us; we have wronged no one, we have corrupted no one, we have taken advantage of no one. I do not say this to condemn you, for I said before that you are in our hearts, to die together and to live together. I often boast about you; I have great pride in you; I am filled with consolation; I am overjoyed in all our affliction. (2 Cor 6:11-12, 7:2-4)

This is a man who suffers for his ministry.

DO WE STILL NEED ST PAUL?

2.   PHYSICAL TRIALS

These are immense (1 Cor 4:11-13; 2 Cor 4:8-10, 6:3-10, 11:23-29, 12:10; Rom 8:35; Gal 4:12-15) and it is only when they are all tabulated that one appreciates the cost of discipleship for Paul:

> To the present hour we are hungry and thirsty, we are poorly clothed and beaten and homeless, and we grow weary from the work of our own hands. When reviled, we bless; when persecuted, we endure; when slandered, we speak kindly. We have become like the rubbish of the world, the dregs of all things, to this very day. (1 Cor 4:11-13)

> We are afflicted in every way, but not crushed; perplexed, but not driven to despair; persecuted, but not forsaken; struck down, but not destroyed; always carrying in the body the death of Jesus, so that the life of Jesus may also be made visible in our bodies. (2 Cor 4:8-10)

> We are putting no obstacle in anyone's way, so that no fault may be found with our ministry, but as servants of God we have commended ourselves in every way: through great endurance, in afflictions, hardships, calamities, beatings, imprisonments, riots, labours, sleepless nights, hunger; by purity, knowledge, patience, kindness, holiness of spirit, genuine love, truthful speech, and the power of God; with the weapons of righteousness for the right hand and for the left; in honour and dishonour, in ill repute and good repute. We are treated as impostors, and yet are true; as unknown, and yet are well known; as dying, and see – we are alive; as punished, and yet not killed; as sorrowful, yet always rejoicing; as poor, yet making

many rich; as having nothing, and yet possessing everything. (2 Cor 6:3-10)

Are they ministers of Christ? I am talking like a madman – I am a better one: with far greater labours, far more imprisonments, with countless floggings, and often near death. Five times I have received from the Jews the forty lashes minus one. Three times I was beaten with rods. Once I received a stoning. Three times I was shipwrecked; for a night and a day I was adrift at sea; on frequent journeys, in danger from rivers, danger from bandits, danger from my own people, danger from Gentiles, danger in the city, danger in the wilderness, danger at sea, danger from false brothers and sisters; in toil and hardship, through many a sleepless night, hungry and thirsty, often without food, cold and naked. And, besides other things, I am under daily pressure because of my anxiety for all the churches. Who is weak, and I am not weak? Who is made to stumble, and I am not indignant? (2 Cor 11:23-29)

Therefore I am content with weaknesses, insults, hardships, persecutions, and calamities for the sake of Christ; for whenever I am weak, then I am strong. (2 Cor 12:10)

Who will separate us from the love of Christ? Will hardship, or distress, or persecution, or famine, or nakedness, or peril, or sword? (Rom 8:35)

Friends, I beg you, become as I am, for I also have become as you are. You have done me no wrong. You know that it was because of a physical infirmity that I first announced the gospel to you; though my condition

put you to the test, you did not scorn or despise me, but
welcomed me as an angel of God, as Christ Jesus. (Gal
4:12-15)

The words speaks for themselves. We know from the travels that Paul
was energetic, fit and hard-working. From these lists of physical trials
we see why he needed to be so physically and psychologically strong.

3.   APOSTOLIC TRIALS

By apostolic trials I mean all the challenges he experienced as an
apostle and as a missionary. Primary among those must be the stress
of the dealings with Peter and the Jerusalem pillars (Acts 15 and
Galatians 2). The confrontation was for the sake of the Gospel of
inclusion, of course, but it caused pain to have to do it.

Paul's own practice of setting up communities and then moving
on to found more brought with it its own loss and grief, as may be
seen in the dealings with Thessalonica and Corinth. The
sustainability of communities under stress was a constant anxiety.
Added to that was the fact that others sometimes arrived and
distorted either the Gospel or the spirituality of the believers. This
clearly happened in Galatia with the arrival of the 'super apostles', as
he sarcastically calls them. But it also happened in Corinth and there
it led to the distorted evaluation of the spectacular spiritual gifts.

In a culture which prized public speaking, Paul falls short in
brilliance. He can turn this to his advantage, but clearly it causes him
pain as well:

I do not want to seem as though I am trying to frighten
you with my letters. For they say, 'His letters are
weighty and strong, but his bodily presence is weak, and
his speech contemptible'. (2 Cor 10:9-10)

Paul can turn this around; nevertheless, it was a block to his work as
a communicator. He might even be, as Jerome Murphy-O'Connor
suggests, the 'thorn in the flesh' of 2 Corinthians 12.

4. EMOTIONAL TRIALS

We have seen above some cases of exceptional anxiety. In one or two places, Paul is very frank about what he has been through as a missionary:

> When I came to Troas to proclaim the good news of Christ, a door was opened for me in the Lord; but my mind could not rest because I did not find my brother Titus there. So I said farewell to them and went on to Macedonia. (2 Cor 2:12-13)

> We do not want you to be unaware, brothers and sisters, of the affliction we experienced in Asia; for we were so utterly, unbearably crushed that we despaired of life itself. Indeed, we felt that we had received the sentence of death so that we would rely not on ourselves but on God who raises the dead. He who rescued us from so deadly a peril will continue to rescue us; on him we have set our hope that he will rescue us again, as you also join in helping us by your prayers, so that many will give thanks on our behalf for the blessing granted us through the prayers of many. (2 Cor 1:8-11)

A particular sadness came from the absence of most Jews from the Christian movement:

> I am speaking the truth in Christ – I am not lying; my conscience confirms it by the Holy Spirit – I have great sorrow and unceasing anguish in my heart. For I could wish that I myself were accursed and cut off from Christ for the sake of my own people, my kindred according to the flesh. (Rom 9:1-3)

5. SUFFERING AND HIS OWN SPIRITUAL JOURNEY

In one place Paul speaks of his own prayer regarding suffering. A little context is necessary. The Corinthians are impressed not only by rhetoric, but also by 'pedigree' and by ecstatic spiritual experiences. In a highly ironic way, Paul gives them what they want while at the same time denying it can have any significance. He establishes his apostolic pedigree in 2 Corinthians 11:16-23. He undermines constantly the affirmation – a very risky tack expertly navigated by the rhetorically brilliant Paul.

He comes finally to his spiritual experiences. In 2 Corinthians 12:1-7, extraordinary religious experiences are recounted. He writes in the third person, a technique of distancing, in case they should think it was an achievement of his or that he attached undue importance to such things. He repeatedly says 'whether in the body or out of the body, I do not know – God knows'. Clearly, these experiences matter greatly to him; yet he does not want their faith to depend on his revelations.

To moderate further his presentations of such 'exceptional revelations', he describes a particular issue, the famous 'thorn in the flesh'. What this was remains opaque. I incline to the hypothesis of Murphy-O'Connor because it is hard to imagine Paul being so preoccupied except for something that affected the ministry. Because it got in the way of the apostolate, he brought it into prayer no less than three times. In prayer, the Lord tells him that 'my grace is enough for you'. This means that Paul himself is now invited to share in the cross of Jesus and so his suffering becomes a means of making present and real the Gospel of the crucified Christ, in the lives of his hearers. Just as before he had to love them so that they would experience the love of God through him, now he bears suffering, so that they may see in him the paradoxical Gospel of God's strength revealed in weakness. This may very well be what he means in Galatians by 'I am crucified with Christ', where he writes in a very focused and dense way:

We ourselves are Jews by birth and not Gentile sinners; yet we know that a person is justified not by the works of the law but through faith in Jesus Christ. And we have come to believe in Christ Jesus, so that we might be justified by faith in Christ, and not by doing the works of the law, because no one will be justified by the works of the law. But if, in our effort to be justified in Christ, we ourselves have been found to be sinners, is Christ then a servant of sin? Certainly not! But if I build up again the very things that I once tore down, then I demonstrate that I am a transgressor. For through the law I died to the law, so that I might live to God. I have been crucified with Christ; and it is no longer I who live, but it is Christ who lives in me. And the life I now live in the flesh I live by faith in the Son of God, who loved me and gave himself for me. I do not nullify the grace of God; for if justification comes through the law, then Christ died for nothing. (Gal 2:15-21)

This is a quite personal confession and, as mentioned before, it is the only time that Paul says Christ loved him. It mirrors closely his paradoxical summary of the Gospel in 1 Corinthians 1:

For the message about the cross is foolishness to those who are perishing, but to us who are being saved it is the power of God. For it is written, 'I will destroy the wisdom of the wise, and the discernment of the discerning I will thwart'. Where is the one who is wise? Where is the scribe? Where is the debater of this age? Has not God made foolish the wisdom of the world? For since, in the wisdom of God, the world did not know God through wisdom, God decided, through the foolishness of our proclamation, to save those who believe. For Jews demand signs and Greeks desire wisdom, but we proclaim Christ crucified, a stumbling

block to Jews and foolishness to Gentiles, but to those
who are the called, both Jews and Greeks, Christ the
power of God and the wisdom of God. (1:18-24)

Paul was a man who knew suffering from the inside out. For him, it
took different dimensions: inter-personal, vocational, physical,
psychological and spiritual. His final answer for himself is that his
suffering aligns him to Jesus for the sake of the Gospel and makes his
preaching credible.

Chapter 9

PRAYER IN THE SPIRIT

It is, perhaps, not too much to say that today we have a crisis of Church but not a crisis of spirituality. The quest for a spiritual path has, for many, widened beyond the Christian tradition. Nevertheless, Christians quite naturally look to their foundational texts for guidance and nourishment. In this chapter, we will focus on what we can learn about prayer from some passages in St Paul. From his own hand and in his own voice, we know about his spiritual experiences and his practical teaching on prayer. Both categories – experience and prayer – present challenges, and so there cannot be any naïve 'reading off the page'. In dealing with ultimate mystery, clarity is not only not attainable, it may not even be desirable.

We begin, as always, with our own time, with its own challenges. It is difficult to name what is happening. The rich variety of devotional practices has waned since Vatican II, which encouraged a more direct experience of the Scriptures and a more conscious participation in liturgy. Devotional practices survive but more on the margins. The charismatic movement came and brought its own gift and energy. For many people, it unlocked prayer as a real, joy-filled relationship. At least for Catholics, it brought a new familiarity, even intimacy, with the Word of God, and above all an awareness of the Spirit praying within. This latter was often evidenced in the more extrovert spiritual gifts, such as prophecy and tongues, but by no means confined to that. It too has waned somewhat, although it still continues as lively as ever in some places. In the last two decades, two more lasting spiritual movements have been evident, and while neither is overwhelmingly popular, they both show the marks of something deep and at the same time accessible to everyone.

The first of these is sacred reading or *lectio divina*. This is a reflective and prayerful reading of Scripture. It is based on the conviction that our life experience can enable the scriptures to speak and that the scriptures can shed light on our life experience. Very often, individuals and groups practising *lectio divina* choose the next Sunday's Gospel from the lectionary. There is a double advantage in this. First of all, the biblical passage is given objectively and not simply chosen from the familiar or the favourite. In the second place, it changes our listening at the Liturgy of the Word (and incidentally, it raises expectations for the homily!). It has the advantage of being quite personal and so nourishing a relationship with Jesus and God's Word. It is also practical and concrete in that it takes place at the level of each participant and promotes discipleship and the ever-present invitation to conversion.

The second of these is the practice of Christian meditation. In essence, meditation is both simple and difficult. It is simple in that all you 'do' is sit in the presence of God, keeping your attention on God's presence through a prayer-word or mantra. There are different approaches, of course, but often the prayer-word is *Lord Jesus Christ, have mercy on me a sinner.* By means of a consistent commitment to this practice, the pray-er begins a spiritual 'mystery tour', a key element of which will be the laying aside your plans and expectations for the journey. If I were to hazard a guess, I would say that the 'future church' will be made of people committed to some kind of relationship with God through meditation, praying with Scripture, participation in worship and transformation both personal and social.

Renewal in the Church has many facets, including institutional reform. Any regeneration is going to include a renewed teaching on the spiritual journey, and at the centre of that, as we have seen about, is relationship. Benedict XVI put it very well in his first encyclical:

> We have come to believe in God's love: in these words
> the Christian can express the fundamental decision of
> his life. Being Christian is not the result of an ethical

choice or a lofty idea, but the encounter with an event, a person, which gives life a new horizon and a decisive direction. Saint John's Gospel describes that event in these words: 'God so loved the world that he gave his only Son, that whoever believes in him should … have eternal life' (3:16). *God is love* §1.

When we turn to St Paul, we find that encounter and relationship stand at the very centre of his experience and teaching on prayer. The fact that he alludes only rarely to it says nothing about its importance:

> For you have heard of my former way of life in Judaism, how I was savagely persecuting the church of God and trying to destroy it. I was advancing in Judaism beyond many of my contemporaries in my nation, and was extremely zealous for the traditions of my ancestors. *But when the one who set me apart from birth and called me by his grace was pleased to reveal his Son in me so that I could preach him among the Gentiles,* I did not go to ask advice from any human being, nor did I go up to Jerusalem to see those who were apostles before me, but right away I departed to Arabia, and then returned to Damascus. (Gal 1:13-17; emphasis added)

Combined with the interior experience of the Spirit, this encounter with Christ risen from the dead constitutes for Paul the heart of the Christian way. This presents a particular challenge to anyone practising and teaching prayer. A personal encounter cannot be conjured up but must simply be awaited, in great stillness and openness. It remains a gift, a grace. A good summary of what is involved is given in Roman 5, where we read:

> Therefore, since we have been declared righteous by faith, we have peace with God through our Lord Jesus

Christ, through whom we have also obtained access by faith into this grace in which we stand, and we rejoice in the hope of God's glory. Not only this, but we also rejoice in sufferings, knowing that suffering produces endurance, and endurance, character, and character, hope. And hope does not disappoint, because the love of God has been poured out in our hearts through the Holy Spirit who was given to us. (Rom 5:1-5)

The prayer of Paul is joy-filled and grateful. This may be seen from any of the thanksgiving prayer with which most of his letters begin. The letter to the Philippians, written late in his life, can serve as an example:

I thank my God every time I remember you. I always pray with joy in my every prayer for all of you because of your participation in the gospel from the first day until now. For I am sure of this very thing, that the one who began a good work in you will perfect it until the day of Christ Jesus. For it is right for me to think this about all of you, because I have you in my heart, since both in my imprisonment and in the defence and confirmation of the gospel all of you became partners in God's grace together with me. For God is my witness that I long for all of you with the affection of Christ Jesus. And I pray this, that your love may abound even more and more in knowledge and every kind of insight so that you can decide what is best, and thus be sincere and blameless for the day of Christ, filled with the fruit of righteousness that comes through Jesus Christ to the glory and praise of God. (Phil 1:3-11)

Paul is writing as an old man and from prison. In spite of these circumstances, the message of the letter is one full of joy and life. It would be an enriching exercise to read the other thanksgiving prayers as well (Rom 1:8-15; 1 Cor 1:4-9; 2 Cor 1:3-11; 1 Thess 1:2-10; Philem 4–7).

Thanksgiving is a foundational prayer in Judaism and Paul remains in this respect a faithful Jew. As we have seen earlier, his ministry and his relationship with his communities are not somehow extraneous to his relationship with God. On the contrary, the Thessalonian, Philippian, Corinthian, Galatian and Roman communities are an integral part of his relationship with God in Christ. He loves them in Christ, and for them he praises God and prays to God. He puts it beautifully in the thanksgiving in Philippians: *I have you in my heart.* The constancy of Paul's prayer for those who accepted his preaching is found also in the very first letter to survive:

> We always give thanks to God for all of you and mention you in our prayers, constantly remembering before our God and Father your work of faith and labour of love and steadfastness of hope in our Lord Jesus Christ. (1 Thess 1:2-3)

Because they are so much part of his life in God, Paul also intercedes for his communities:

> Now may God our Father himself and our Lord Jesus direct our way to you. And may the Lord cause you to increase and abound in love for one another and for all, just as we do for you, so that your hearts are strengthened in holiness to be blameless before our God and Father at the coming of our Lord Jesus with all his saints. (1 Thess 3:11-13)

Within the formal thanksgiving sections of his letters, Paul singles out the gifts of the particular community for special thanks. This includes of course their faith, hope and love, their courage and so forth. It also includes their experience of the Spirit, as we read:

We know, brothers and sisters loved by God, that he has chosen you, in that our gospel did not come to you merely in words, but in power and in the Holy Spirit and with deep conviction (surely you recall the character we displayed when we came among you to help you). (1 Thess 1:4-5)

For you were made rich in every way in him, in all your speech and in every kind of knowledge – just as the testimony about Christ has been confirmed among you – so that you do not lack any spiritual gift as you wait for the revelation of our Lord Jesus Christ. (1 Cor 1:5-7)

There was a special problem in Corinth on account of the exuberance of the Spirit's gifts and the somewhat distorted attachment of the Corinthians to the more flashy gifts. The most extended discussion of the use and abuse of the gifts takes place in 1 Corinthians 12–14. In the end, Paul affirms the gifts of the Spirit, but prefers more rational discourse: *I thank God that I speak in tongues more than all of you, but in the church I want to speak five words with my mind to instruct others, rather than ten thousand words in a tongue* (1 Cor 14:18-19).

In Galatians, where there is no thanksgiving because Paul is too upset, the experience of the Spirit is presumed and can be pointed to as an argument that the Law, imposed on the Galatians by outsiders, brought nothing extra:

The only thing I want to learn from you is this: Did you receive the Spirit by doing the works of the law or by believing what you heard? Are you so foolish? Although you began with the Spirit, are you now trying to finish by human effort? Have you suffered so many things for nothing? – if indeed it was for nothing. Does God then give you the Spirit and work miracles among you by your doing the works of the law or by your believing what you heard? (Gal 3:2-5)

Towards the close of that letter, he urges them warmly:

> But the fruit of the Spirit is love, joy, peace, patience, kindness, goodness, faithfulness, gentleness, and self-control. Against such things there is no law. Now those who belong to Christ have crucified the flesh with its passions and desires. If we live by the Spirit, let us also behave in accordance with the Spirit. (Gal 5:22-26)

This *experience* of the Spirit is a vital part of the Pauline proclamation. Those who heard him deeply received that Spirit; they were empowered to pray in a way which unlocked their hearts; the great qualities listed in Galatians became a reality for them. It was not only tongues and prophecy and interpretation which were evidence of the Spirit. The Spirit was also active in the everyday living out of the Gospel. The great hymn in 1 Corinthians 13 makes it clear that there is no higher gift than love and this gift is not reserved for an elite but is the mark of all who follow Christ. As we see elsewhere, such love is the heart of the teaching of Jesus and the heart of the teaching of Paul. The poetry in 1 Corinthians is meant to move hearts and minds. Nevertheless, the living of love happens in the prose of the everyday. The teaching of Jesus is clear:

> Jesus answered, 'The most important is: "*Listen, Israel, the Lord our God, the Lord is one. Love the Lord your God with all your heart, with all your soul, with all your mind, and with all your strength.*" The second is: "*Love your neighbour as yourself.*"' (Mk 12:29-31)

In the heavenly hymn to love, Paul repeats the earthly/earthy teaching of Jesus, as we can see elsewhere in his letters:

DO WE STILL NEED ST PAUL?

For the whole law can be summed up in a single commandment, namely, *'You must love your neighbour as yourself.'* (Gal 5:14-15)

Owe no one anything, except to love one another, for the one who loves his neighbour has fulfilled the law. For the commandments, *'Do not commit adultery, do not murder, do not steal, do not covet,'* (and if there is any other commandment) are summed up in this, *'Love your neighbour as yourself.'* Love does no wrong to a neighbour. Therefore love is the fulfilment of the law. (Rom 13:8-10)

But this perhaps less spectacular gift is ours because the love of God has been poured into our hearts by the Holy Spirit.

The Holy Spirit is named often in the Pauline letters. The most penetrating reflection is to be found in Romans 8, one of the most thrilling passages from the pen of St Paul. Where Paul places a reflection affects its purpose and function. In Romans 1–4, as noted earlier, Paul tries to unsettle Jewish and Gentile Christians in their attitudes of superiority, one over the other. This is achieved by reminding both sides of their moral failure and their need of God's grace. In Romans 5–8, Paul turns to that very grace of God and he lists, more or less in chronological order, all that the Roman Christians have received as a gift in Christ. There is an implied rhetorical question: with all this in common, how can there be divisions?

The list begins in Romans 5, with an exposition on salvation in Christ, followed by faith. He goes on in Romans 6 to reflect on baptism and its potential for the believer. Romans 7 is a passage requiring careful exposition; in any case, at one level Paul is not ignoring the reality of the moral struggle even after faith and baptism. That chapter ends with an anguished plea:

Wretched man that I am! Who will rescue me from this body of death? Thanks be to God through Jesus Christ our Lord! So then, I myself serve the law of God with my mind, but with my flesh I serve the law of sin. (Rom 7:24-25)

The second sentence anticipates the truly tremendous confidence so richly explored and exposed in Romans 8. The last section has an underlying trinitarian framework: in prayer, we can call God, Abba, Father; the Holy Spirit helps us in our weakness; the victory of Christ engenders an unshakeable hope in the believer. Thus, chapter 8 combines the sense of excitement from 5:1-5 with the realism of Romans 7. At the experiential heart of this chapter is the Spirit, the Holy Spirit from God, poured out into our hearts.

A major affirmation is found in Romans 8:

You, however, are not in the flesh but in the Spirit, if indeed the Spirit of God lives in you. Now if anyone does not have the Spirit of Christ, this person does not belong to him. But if Christ is in you, your body is dead because of sin, but the Spirit is your life because of righteousness. Moreover if the Spirit of the one who raised Jesus from the dead lives in you, the one who raised Christ from the dead will also make your mortal bodies alive through his Spirit who lives in you. (Rom 8:9-11)

Paul prepares the hearer for this wonderful affirmation in three moments. The first moment in Rom 8:1-2 is really a résumé of Romans 5, viewed as an objective reality. The language is carefully chosen to reflect the achievement of Romans 2–4. A more subjective, existentialist account of that reality is given in Rom 8:5-8, where two worlds, two ways of living are contrasted. Bridging the objective and the subjective is the brief expansion in Rom 8:3-4. The events of salvation took place so that we might walk not according to the flesh, but according to the Spirit. There follows the resounding affirmation of vv. 9–11. Beneath the balanced phrases and the careful theology stands a quietly exultant realisation, as if the reality of the Christ event has burst on Paul again for the first time!

The affirmation of the Spirit's presence is a matter of faith; it is also foundational. At the same time, it is not just *any* spirit of God who dwells in us: it is the Spirit of Christ, even the Spirit of him who raised Christ from the dead, who lives in us. Paul follows this exultant moment with a renewed recognition of reality: as a result we are obligated to live according to this very same Spirit.

Just as Paul is careful to keep his affirmation grounded in the Christ event, likewise he is careful to register this spiritual affirmation in the actual prayer of the believer. From Jesus the early Christians received the word Abba, his word for God. For the first generation of believers, there was an immensely strong sense of being a child of God. By evoking that whole sense of adoption and intimacy, Paul 'proves' to the Romans in their actual lived experience the truth of what he has been claiming. To repeat, the message is that our communion in such deep reality renders irrelevant the (human) issues which are causing divisions among the Roman Christians. Already here, the identity of believers as heirs and even co-heirs anticipates the triumphal hymn to victory which closes Romans 8.

Having established the interiority of the Spirit, Paul now moves to the big picture of world history. Here the language is explicitly apocalyptic, as we see from the use of the word apocalypse, as both verb (Rom 8:18) and noun (Rom 8:19). The imagery may seem a little remote to us – the cosmos giving birth, in a great maternal metaphor – yet again Paul's aim is to stay close to and to interpret experience. In general, apocalyptic writing affirms two things. First of all, it recognises the current challenge to faith in God, the experience of suffering (futility, bondage, decay, groans, suffering). It is especially sharp for the believer in Christ: why are things *still* like this? Secondly, apocalyptic imagery interprets the current experience of suffering not simply as something we must endure until the better comes but even more as the beginning of the end, the first instalment, the labour pains which announce and facilitate the birth (eagerly waiting, children of God, the first fruits, adoption, redemption of our bodies). Faith as Paul presents it is neither 'cheap' nor escapist. Hope is grounded in reality, calling for endurance.

> For in hope we were saved. Now hope that is seen is not hope, because who hopes for what he sees? But if we hope for what we do not see, we eagerly wait for it with endurance. (Rom 8:24-25)

Paul then immediately takes the readers back from the big picture to the experience of the Spirit.

> In the same way, the Spirit helps us in our weakness, for we do not know how we should pray, but the Spirit himself intercedes for us with inexpressible groanings. And he who searches our hearts knows the mind of the Spirit, because the Spirit intercedes on behalf of the saints according to God's will. (Rom 8:26-28)

Even the great Paul does not claim to know how to pray – in spite of conversion, his encounter with the risen Lord, his many experiences of miracles and the manifestations of the Spirit. Prayer is simply not a human achievement. Prayer, the experience of the beyond in the midst, happens at another level altogether. The Spirit lives within and the practice of prayer is a gradual setting aside our agenda for this relationship, and a deepening assent to the Spirit within. We need not be anxious about the quality of our prayer, for the Spirit intercedes according to God's will. It is sufficient to know this is true and to live accordingly. Again, the modesty of Paul's personal claim, the setting aside of anything elitist, serves to call the Roman Christians away from fractious rivalry and back to faith-filled reality.

Spiritual realities are not our doing and no special merit can be claimed. All is gift, all is grace.

The difficult train of thought is suddenly lightened by a special rhetorical figure, that of *sorites*, in which the closing word of one phrase provides the opening word of the next (it comes from the Greek meaning 'to heap up'). There is an emotional climax in the figure which serves Paul's purpose.

> And we know that all things work together for good for those who love God, who are called according to his purpose, because those whom he *foreknew* he also *predestined* to be conformed to the image of his Son, that his Son would be the firstborn among many brothers and sisters. And those he *predestined*, he also called; and those he *called*, he also justified; and those he justified, he also *glorified*. (Rom 8:28-30; emphasis added)

Three different kinds of words are used here: apocalyptic (all things work for good; foreknew, predestined, glorified); Jewish identity from the Torah (justified); Christian discipleship (love God, image, firstborn, brothers and sisters). Even in the lighter literary vein of *sorites*, Paul's three worlds are present: an apocalyptic Jew, who believed in Christ.

The literary tone of the latter few verses continues even more richly in the final verses of chapter 8.

> What then shall we say about these things? If God is for us, who can be against us? Indeed, he who did not spare his own Son, but gave him up for us all – how will he not also, along with him, freely give us all things? Who will bring any charge against God's elect? It is God who justifies. Who is the one who will condemn? Christ is the one who died (and more than that, he was raised),

who is at the right hand of God, and who also is interceding for us. Who will separate us from the love of Christ? Will trouble, or distress, or persecution, or famine, or nakedness, or danger, or sword? As it is written, 'For your sake we encounter death all day long; we were considered as sheep to be slaughtered.' No, in all these things we have complete victory through him who loved us! For I am convinced that neither death, nor life, nor angels, nor heavenly rulers, nor things that are present, nor things to come, nor powers, nor height, nor depth, nor anything else in creation will be able to separate us from the love of God in Christ Jesus our Lord. (Rom 8:31-39)

At the start, Paul is proceeding with rhetorical questions, questions which need no answer because we all know the answer. Let me propose one small change in the above translation. In verse 34 we read: Who is the one who will condemn? Christ is the one who died (and more than that, he was raised), who is at the right hand of God, and who also is interceding for us (Rom 8:34-35). This might more sensibly be translated in the form of a question as, 'Is it Christ, the one who died etc.?' leading to another implied and even stronger, 'of course not'.

The chapter ends with the love of God in Christ, mediated as we saw, through the presence of gift of the Spirit. The ending fittingly echoes both the start of chapter 8 itself and at the same time the start of the whole argument in Romans 5–8.

There is therefore now no condemnation for those who are in Christ Jesus. For the law of the life-giving Spirit in Christ Jesus has set you free from the law of sin and death. (Rom 8:1-2)

Therefore, since we have been declared righteous by faith, we have peace with God through our Lord Jesus

Christ, through whom we have also obtained access by faith into this grace in which we stand, and we rejoice in the hope of God's glory. Not only this, but we also rejoice in *sufferings*, knowing that *suffering* produces *endurance*, and *endurance, character,* and *character, hope.* And hope does not disappoint, because the love of God has been poured out in our hearts through the Holy Spirit who was given to us. (Rom 5:1-5; emphasis added)

The attentive reader will notice once more the figure of *sorites*, in the extract above, forming a frame with its re-use in 8:28-30.

Paul's teaching on the Spirit in Romans 8 has a special appeal today. The big picture he paints is attractive, both existentially and ecologically. Somehow, everything is one and the Spirit breathes in all. At the same time, the groundedness of Paul may be worth underlining. It is not just *any* spirit which is given to us nor is our experience immediately an experience of the universal spirit of all religions. On the contrary, it is the Spirit of Christ, the Spirit of him who raised Jesus from the dead, who is given to us. The Christ event, with all its 'scandalous particularity', is *the event*, the happening which marks out the Christian.

This link with the reality of Christ is matched by a link with the reality of Christians. We do suffer. We are pulled two ways. We live by faith, not by sight (2 Cor 5:7). Our journey is one of tenacious transformation, the never-ending conversion of heart and mind and self. Even in Romans 8, Paul continually keeps us grounded by returning again and again, amidst exhilarating affirmations of faith, to reality, to the mundane and the everyday. If salvation is to happen at all, this is where it has to happen. Not for nothing is the word love present at the start of Romans 5 (vv. 5 and 8) and the end of Romans 8 (vv. 28, 35, 37, 39). *And now faith, hope, and love abide, these three; and the greatest of these is love* (1 Cor 13:13). Thus Paul brings the core teaching of Jesus himself to bear on the Roman Christians and on us today.

Paul's concern to balance the visionary and the practical remains our concern today. Many people find that Christian meditation brings an experience of the Spirit within and that the commitment to such quiet prayer allows 'Abba, Father' to well up from within. At the same time, the practice of *lectio divina* serves to keep our spiritual journey grounded in both the Word of God and actual lived experience. The challenge of the Word keeps conversion before our eyes. In the end, we cannot separate the love of God from the love of the neighbour. This is the core teaching of Jesus and repeated by Paul. It remains our challenge today.

Paul is something of a poet in Romans 8. It may be fitting to cite another poet to close this chapter. Gerard Manley Hopkins gets the Pauline juxtaposition of the visionary and the real just about right, in these words.

> In a flash, at a trumpet crash,
> I am all at once what Christ is, since he was what I am,
> and
> This Jack, jóke, poor pótsherd, patch, matchwood,
> immortal diamond,
> Is immortal diamond.

Chapter 10

PAUL AS PASTOR[1]

When we begin to look to the New Testament for perspectives on pastoral practice, immediately Paul comes to mind. Why Paul? Other documents of the New Testament are of course also pastoral, but only in Paul do we have such a variety of documents, revealing his approaches and strategies in a range of contexts. In other New Testament documents, the personality of the writer is embedded somewhat in the implied author, whereas with Paul we have his actual words to communities in concrete circumstances. As a result, we feel we know more about the personality of the historical Paul than any of the other New Testament writers, many of whom, in any case, are anonymous.

But there are challenges, as well as opportunities, in reading the surviving documents from Paul as a way of gaining insight from his pastoral policies. His world is very different from ours. Often feminist criticism comes to the fore – but it is not the only issue. Politically, he lives in the golden age of the Roman *imperium*. Culturally, he is a bilingual Jew living in the Greco-Roman world, mostly the eastern Mediterranean. Religiously, he is a messianic apocalyptic Jew, expecting soon the final judgement of God on human history. In a word, his religious world is very different to ours, and not just his religious world, but his world *tout court*. Biblical studies often begin with a process of defamiliarisation, as a way not only of establishing the task of interpretation, but also as a way of locating the documents in the historical, cultural and religious contexts. He lived, of course,

1 An earlier version of this chapter appeared as 'Paul as Pastor' in Doctrine and Life, 55 (2005), pp. 45–59.

before psychology and the whole raft of human sciences which we use to enable us critically to reflect upon and fine-tune our engagement with our world. Well you might wonder if we could learn from such a person.

Not less daunting is the fact that our only real evidence for how Paul functioned is the seven letters, commonly regarded as the authentic letters. There is some material in Acts, but even apart from clashes of chronology, the material in Acts seems to be somewhat stylised and even idealised. It is not without interest that Acts reports the conversion of Paul no less than three times, a measure of the anxiety generated by this unruly charismatic figure, both indispensable and dangerous. The letters, at first blush, freeze a moment in a larger conversation. But, fortunately, they do contain, broadly speaking, the wider narrative of relationship, which helps us reconstruct in some measure not only the presenting issues, but the overall context and the typical approaches. What happened to the letters once delivered we don't really know, except to say they were preserved, which can be read to mean they were successful. It is the wider narrative frame that permits us to reconstruct a picture of Paul's pastoral practice in a range of settings, illustrating a variety of concerns and revealing both a coherent strategy and contingent responses. In the course of this chapter, we will travel to Thessalonica, Corinth and Rome.

Before taking flight, we need some idea of the time frame. Following on what was said in the first chapter, Paul was born in Tarsus (Cilicia) probably around 6 BC. After his conversion in around AD 34 to 37, he went to Arabia for a year and then spent about five years in Damascus. The fourteen years from 37 to 51 were spent evangelising in Syria and Cilicia, the centre of the mission being Antioch. Paul implies some kind of outreach also to Asia Minor (Turkey). The letters begin to be written towards the end of that period. All this means that before we see any letter of Paul, he has been involved with Christianity both as a convert and a missionary for almost twenty years. The letters illustrate the latter stage of Paul's career when he began to move westward, towards Rome and Spain.

Paul, of course, has a strategy as an evangelist in terms of both a guiding idea and an actual plan of how to put it into effect. The guiding idea is the extension of salvation, by means of Jesus' death and resurrection, to include all humanity, the joining together in one people of God both Jews and Gentiles. It is vital to his interest to avoid two possible pitfalls in nascent Christianity. The pitfall is the temptation to insist that all identity markers of the people of the first covenant should be insisted upon, in particular the dietary laws, feast days and circumcision. He encounters this problem in his first missionary centre in Antioch where he has to go to some trouble to oppose Cephas and the conservative elements in Jerusalem. The second danger is to cut the child (belief in Jesus as Messiah) off entirely from its parent form (Judaism). This disjunction is a constant threat in Christianity, which has the difficult task of proclaiming something new while insisting upon continuity and fulfilment. (That it is not merely an ancient temptation may be seen from the number of people who wonder why we do not simply ditch the Old Testament altogether.) The first risk is political: the movement would have remained an ethnically centred phenomenon of no great significance. The second risk is theological: God would have shown himself inconsistent not only in his dealings with humanity, but even with himself. (The dark side of failing to recognise continuity with and the continued validity of the first covenant is Christian anti-Semitism.) The very practical project of the Jerusalem collection for Judean Christians is not only an economic support to the Church in need but a living symbol of the two lungs breathing in the body of Christ. This is but one of the techniques by which Paul portrays, in a tangible way, his vision of a unified humanity.

At the heart of his proclamation stand the death and resurrection of Jesus. For Paul, this is a proclamation of liberation and the gift of a new way of being. It is liberation, in his language, from sin, death, the Law and from exclusion from the Covenant. Positively stated, it is forgiveness and love, resurrection, the freedom of the children of God (Rom 8:21) and, not least, the inclusion of the Gentiles. The corollary is a new way of being. As Paul puts it, in Christ we are a new creation: the God who made the world acted in Christ with the same power, or rather with even more power, in the resurrection (2 Cor 2:4-6). Suddenly, all distinctions are abolished: 'There is no longer Jew or Greek, there is no longer slave or free, there is no longer male and female; for all of you are one in Christ Jesus' (Gal 3:28). The abolition of socially constructed distinctions is radical and challenging. Even for the individual, there is to be a new way of life, which cannot be legislated for: 'By contrast, the fruit of the Spirit is love, joy, peace, patience, kindness, generosity, faithfulness, gentleness, and self-control. There is no law against such things' (Gal 5:22-23). In the same letter to the Galatians, putting it very plainly, he writes: 'For freedom Christ has set us free' (Gal 5:1). In the ministry, it was hard not only for his hearers to act consistently with this revolution – even Paul is not always consistent with himself. For the sake of credibility, he had, of course, to embody the proclamation in his ministry, to make it tangible in his person. He was their only experience of the Gospel. So, how does he operate as a pastor?

First of all, he works with a team. This is apparent from the opening greetings in five of the seven authentic letters. I suppose it would be cumbersome to say 'A reading from the first letter of Paul and Sosthenes to the Corinthians' but that *is* how it starts. The other four are all from both Paul and Timothy. It is not without significance that only the letters to the Galatians and the Romans come, it would seem, from Paul alone. Apart from those mentioned by name in the letters, Paul has many collaborators. Of course it is not all sweetness and light. The closeness between Paul and Barnabas, all during the long Antioch ministry, ended in tears. Even among the saints, working with others is not without its stresses and fractures. Nevertheless Paul always has fellow workers, a team he can rely on to keep him in touch with the communities founded by him and carry to them his letters. It is even likely that his letters were discussed among them before being committed to papyrus. And, if you ask what happened when a letter arrived, the example of Galatians may help: it was the task of the bearer to explain the content.

In the second place, he leaves behind a structure, a kind of core group, who will be responsible for the community. This is necessary, given that Paul is in a hurry and wants always to move on, but it is also enabling. This is apparent even in the very first letter to survive, that to the Thessalonians, where he writes:

> But we appeal to you, brothers and sisters, to respect those who labour among you, and have charge of you in the Lord and admonish you; esteem them very highly in love because of their work. (1 Thess 5:12-13)

It is only a passing reference but all the more convincing for that. Famously, he commends Phoebe, deacon of the church in Cenchreae, to the Romans, and he names Junia as an apostle (Rom 16:7). People have asked, of course, what model of community Paul used. The culture offered a number of models: synagogue, voluntary associations, mystery religions and philosophical schools. It seems, however, that the closest model is the more prosaic but more appropriate household. This, very likely, arises directly from the immediate setting of the movement: people's homes. It also helps to ground the language of fictive kinship in the letters: brothers and sisters, father and mother.

Finally, he has a dream of establishing Christian communities in the main cities of the Roman empire – not only in Asia Minor, but also in Europe: Philippi, Thessalonica, Athens, Corinth, Rome itself and even beyond Rome, reaching out to Spain. Writing about this very project in his last letter, Romans, he lets his guard down slightly: 'But now, with no further place for me in these regions, I desire, as I have for many years, to come to you when I go to Spain' (Rom 15:23-24). The eastern Mediterranean is a big place! The little phrase 'with no further place for me in these regions' reveals perhaps some of the root tensions of his ministry as imagined by

Paul. He really does want to found churches where no one else has been. That 'always on the go' attitude is in tension with his highly personalised ministry, by which he embodies in himself, with great energy and love, the Gospel he proclaims. And that, in turn, is in tension with the somewhat awkward character he turned out to be – a founder who moved on but wanted to remain influential. At the same time, he can be emotional, uneven, to put it mildly. It is a kind of triangle: I want to start a new church, I want to be the significant figure in each church, and I am, nevertheless, difficult to get on with. This tense triangle will help us evaluate Paul's ministry in three places: Thessalonica, Corinth and Rome.

Paul himself once said, 'When I am weak, then I am strong'. We know from experience that our strengths are often our weakness. What are the strengths of Paul? Apart from general gifts of energy, resilience and selflessness, I would name three other things. First of all, he brings a passionate faith, grounded in his conversion experience. Second, his desire is to be in the vanguard of evangelisation in the known inhabited world. That is one of the reasons why he wishes never to work where someone else has started. Finally, he brings to bear a formidable intellect, capable of detailed, sometimes obscure, scriptural argument in the service of extraordinarily able, rhetorically subtle persuasion. Each strength betokens a weakness. He is passionate, sometimes very sharp, occasionally unjust and once or twice plain vulgar. Also, his experience of working with other major figures was not happy, and his ability to endure those who follow him in a community is likewise not always happy. You might think at least his intellectual abilities don't cause trouble, but the Corinthians complain that the gap between his shaky oratory and his powerful writings is too great. Even St Peter says there are things in them difficult to understand:

> So also our beloved brother Paul wrote to you according to the wisdom given him, speaking of this as

he does in all his letters. There are some things in them hard to understand, which the ignorant and unstable twist to their own destruction, as they do the other scriptures. (2 Pet 3:16)

How did all this work in practice? The pastoral strategy of Paul, essentially an urban figure, can be illustrated by following him around the three aforementioned locations and noticing what happens to his relationship with Thessalonians, Corinthians and Romans as we go along.

(i) Thessalonica

We travel first to Thessalonica, the capital city of Roman Macedonia, lying in the best natural harbour in all of Greece. It was a thriving city, making full use not only of its advantages as a port, but also of its strategic position on the *Via Egnatia*, the great Roman road crossing northern Greece from the west coast to the east. Not much remains of ancient Thessalonica, but what does gives the impression of a typical Hellenistic city, rich, confident, successful, beautiful. Although arriving into this culture and hoping to make converts to yet another religion from the Middle East was a formidable task, Paul seems to have had remarkable success, which he can point to in the letter, to the credit of the Thessalonians.

In spite of this, the letter is revealing about Paul the pastor, because it is written in some anxiety, not just on account of the presenting issues (which are well known) but also on account of the relationship between Paul and the Thessalonians. Simply put, Paul indeed had startling success in Thessalonica and then, as was his wont, he moved on to Athens and from there to Corinth. His time in Thessalonica had been emotionally intense, both for him and for the Thessalonians, and now his absence and seeming unwillingness to come to them again were being interpreted as loss of attachment and cooling of affection, casting doubt not only on his present feelings, but his past integrity and sincerity.

Paul defends himself in two ways. First of all, he refutes any idea of his unwillingness by claiming that he was prevented from returning to them by no less a figure than Satan. Second, Paul rehearses the history of his mission and then defends his sincerity by recalling his own hard work among them, as he earned his own keep. In an acute observation about Paul the manual labourer, Jerome Murphy-O'Connor notices that Paul speaks of his work as a tentmaker somewhat in the manner of someone born to something better. There is good reason to think that Paul undertook tent-making as a convenient way of supporting himself while on the move around the Mediterranean. Permission to live from the ministry is widely attested in the New Testament.

> Take no gold, or silver, or copper in your belts, no bag for your journey, or two tunics, or sandals, or a staff; for labourers deserve their food. (Mt 10:9-10)

> Remain in the same house, eating and drinking whatever they provide, for the labourer deserves to be paid. Do not move about from house to house. (Lk 10:7)

> Or does he not speak entirely for our sake? It was indeed written for our sake, for whoever ploughs should plough in hope and whoever threshes should thresh in hope of a share in the crop. If we have sown spiritual good among you, is it too much if we reap your material benefits? If others share this rightful claim on you, do not we still more? Nevertheless, we have not made use of this right, but we endure anything rather than put an obstacle in the way of the gospel of Christ. Do you not know that those who are employed in the temple service get their food from the temple, and those who serve at the altar share in what is sacrificed on the altar?

In the same way, the Lord commanded that those who proclaim the gospel should get their living by the gospel. (1 Cor 9:10-14)

Let the elders who rule well be considered worthy of double honour, especially those who labour in preaching and teaching; for the scripture says, 'You shall not muzzle an ox while it is treading out the grain', and, 'The labourer deserves to be paid'. (1 Tim 5:17-18)

A later, rather revealing text confirms the risks attendant upon such open hospitality!

Everyone 'who comes in the name of the Lord' is to be welcomed. But then examine him, and you will find out – for you will have insight – what is true and what is false. If the one who comes is merely passing through, assist him as much as you can. But he must not stay with you for more than two or, if necessary, three days. However, if he wishes to settle among you and is a craftsman, let him work for his living. But if he is not a craftsman, decide according to your own judgement how he shall live among you as a Christian, yet without being idle. But if he does not wish to cooperate in this way, then he is trading on Christ. Beware of such people. But every genuine prophet who wishes to settle among you 'is worthy of his food'. (Didache 12:1–13:1)

And Paul himself says in 1 Thessalonians, he could have leaned on them as an apostle but did not. Of course, it got him into trouble, because in an honour-shame society, reciprocity was a cultural given. You do not simply give – you honour other people by receiving from them too. Conversely, you dishonour by giving only. Why would Paul insist on this?

In actual practice, he seems to have been inconsistent. Mostly, he wishes to be quite independent, but occasionally he takes money, sometimes for the project of the Jerusalem collection, but also sometimes for his own ministry. His wish to be independent can be understood against the flood of charlatans, especially religious and philosophical spiritual swindlers, who were a pest in Greco-Roman cities. Often people accused such itinerant sages of manipulation for financial gain. By not taking any money as a rule, you could kill two birds with the one stone here: you could avoid that accusation and also promote your sincerity and high motivation. I think it also appealed to Paul, as someone from roughly the middle classes, to maintain his independence. Of course there was a cultural clash, and Paul's manner of speaking about it is interesting:

> Though we might have made demands as apostles of Christ. But we were gentle among you, like a nurse tenderly caring for her own children. So deeply do we care for you that we are determined to share with you not only the gospel of God but also our own selves, because you have become very dear to us. (1 Thess 2:7-8)

'We might have made demands' means we could have expected at least our upkeep while staying with you. 'Like a nurse tenderly caring for her own children' is not only charming but also revealing. It is not solely a metaphor of tenderness – for that he could have written, 'like a mother, tenderly caring for her own children'. The point is that a wet nurse receives payment for breast-feeding the children of others – but naturally, when it comes to her own children, she does not, and presumably would not wish to, receive payment. The precision of the metaphor not only puts in perspective any idea of financial gain but also brings to expression an intimacy, within a pastoral relationship, which we would perhaps find disturbing. The intimacy is not simply a literary flourish – he really means it. He speaks of himself as a father and a mother to them. He uses very strong words to speak of his longing to be with them. He describes sharing 'not only the gospel of

God but also our own selves'. He can even reverse the parental imagery and speak of himself feeling like an orphan when separated from them.

Clearly, Paul is someone who does not stint his engagement. Being an apostle is by no means simply a role, but his whole self. When he preaches, he himself models for them the faith (really, the love) he is trying to attract them to. In a sense, he absolutely has to, because otherwise they will have no tangible experience of the Gospel. This is so much the case that he himself, who elsewhere vigorously rejects human boasting, proposes himself as a model to follow: 'And you became imitators of us and of the Lord' (1 Thess 1:6). There is something utterly right about this: the pastoral agent has to be there for the people in a completely personal way, not only talking about the Gospel second hand, by hearsay, but living it and embodying it somehow for the community. But the risks are also apparent. This is not only the risk of attachment to a degree that cannot be fulfilled or maintained. It is also clear, however, that the inability to receive has somewhat disturbed the Thessalonians, because they feel dishonoured. The financial independence is only a symptom: those to whom we give are honoured and acknowledged when we are able to receive from them. Paul lets the cat out of the bag a little in writing to the Romans:

> For I am longing to see you so that I may share with you
> some spiritual gift to strengthen you – or rather so that
> we may be mutually encouraged by each other's faith,
> both yours and mine. (Rom 1:11-12)

The quick recover barely conceals the first inclination, which is to be the giver only. This tendency to be a giver only lands Paul in trouble, simply because he does not respect the cultural convention which honours those one serves by allowing them, too, to be generous givers. There is tension between the modelling of love and the zeal to be elsewhere, just as there is tension between the service and the independence. Nevertheless, Paul is not here in controlling mode – for the very reason of his apostolate to the Gentile, he must *leave* them and leave *them* in charge.

(ii) Corinth

Next, we travel down the east coast of Greece, beyond Athens, and arrive at the capital of Achaia. The present-day ruins of ancient Corinth are still striking and even the casual visitor comes away with the impression of a city that was rich in culture and education, and perfectly positioned for trade. The city at the time of Paul had been revived in 46 BC by order of Julius Caesar, who saw, correctly, the potential of the location. At the time Paul visited, Corinth had between 80–100,000 inhabitants. Again, his mission was successful. In fact, he was almost too successful, because the charismatic gifts, those spectacular and gratifying manifestations of the Spirit, became both common and noisy and threatened ordinary quiet in worship.

Although Paul spent a considerable time in Corinth, nevertheless, it seems he laid only the foundations of the faith. He himself confesses that he actually baptised hardly anyone and that he was obliged to give them only infants' milk. ('I fed you with milk, not solid food, for you were not ready for solid food.' [1 Cor 3:2]) The upshot was that when he again moved on and the local and other evangelists filled the leadership vacuum, they were not only better speakers (as Paul freely admits), but completed and brought to maturity the faith of the Corinthians. One effect was that he became displaced in the affections of the Corinthians; but worse than that, factions had riven the community. Rivalries were already likely because the community was household-based and natural sympathy between friends was bound to have a role, not to mention the part played by class distinctions. You could also ask why Paul would have objected to the fact that others had taken his place? Was it not the very nature of his mission that he should move on and leave structures behind him, which would, as he would naturally wish, bring about the development and maturation of the faith of the Corinthians?

As always, things are more complex. First of all, he is afraid that the Corinthians are too attracted to the spectacular spirituals gifts. Consistent with that, they are also drawn to better speakers, on the false foundation of flashy rhetoric. Furthermore, the community, already household-based, naturally breaks into factions depending on which speaker is found to be more agreeable. 'For it has been reported to me by Chloe's people that there are quarrels among you, my brothers and sisters. What I mean is that each of you says, "I belong to Paul", or "I belong to Apollos", or "I belong to Cephas", or "I belong to Christ"' (1 Cor 1:11-12). As a good pastor, Paul penetrates behind these spiritual and, so to speak, political leanings and sees lurking there an understanding of the Gospel that undermines the proclamation of the risen Christ by overlooking the crucified Christ. The outcome is a misleading attachment to servants of the Gospel, which Paul sets out to undermine:

> What then is Apollos? What is Paul? Servants through whom you came to believe, as the Lord assigned to each. I planted, Apollos watered, but God gave the growth. So neither the one who plants nor the one who waters *is anything,* but only God who gives the growth. (1 Cor 3:5-7; emphasis added)

Although neither the one who plants nor the one who waters *is anything,* nevertheless, he reminds them, using the language of fictive kinship, that they have only one father: 'you do not have many fathers' (perhaps a flash of humour); 'For though you might have ten thousand guardians in Christ, you do not have many fathers. Indeed, in Christ Jesus I became your father through the gospel' (1 Cor 4:15). He may have had to examine his conscience here: the proclamation of orthodoxy brings with it a restoration of his position as authoritative founder of the community, but untrammelled by false modesty, he sees himself as the keystone of orthodoxy. Sometimes you wonder how much he needed to be in charge or at least needed to be the key figure for a community. It may be that his experience in Antioch and Galatia led him to mistrust others who do not enjoy the theological penetration and adamantine clarity of his proclamation. He would claim, at least, that putting himself forward was at the service of the Gospel.

However, in the end he does feel able to recommend Stephanus and other leaders in the community.

(iii) Rome

Rome needs no introduction, except to say that at that time it was easily and by far the largest city in the Roman Empire, with approximately one million inhabitants. Of these, some 50–100,000 were Jews, and it is assumed, rightly I think, that the first news of Jesus arrived through the house synagogues of Rome. The history of the Roman community is not exactly known, but it is assumed that something like this had happened. Initially, the communities were largely Jewish in character, following the customs of the elders with regard to dietary laws, feasts and circumcision. Because of conflict over Christ, Jewish Christians were expelled under the emperor Claudius and the membership of the Christian house churches became largely Gentile in character. These naturally developed in their own way and let drop the distinctive practices of Christian Jews. When the decree of exile was relaxed, the expelled Jews who followed Jesus returned and, understandably I suppose, expected to resume their former position of leadership in the community. Conflict ensued. The Gentile brothers and sisters could rightly claim that they had, in the absence of the Jews, matured in freedom and discovered that aspects of the Law were no longer valid. On the other hand, the Jewish brothers and sisters could rightly claim that the matrix of the Christian movement was Judaism and that the Law, given in all its detail by God on Mount Sinai to Moses, had never been rescinded. To them in this situation Paul writes his longest letters, that to the Romans.

This is a challenge because he cannot claim any founding authority, and perhaps that is why he writes to them at such length, because he, in their eyes at least, is only as good as his arguments. In writing to them, however, he is aware that this conflict in Rome threatens the entire project of his ministry, which was to show that God has now included Gentiles equally in the election, through the death of Jesus, without the precondition of dietary laws, circumcision and the liturgical calendar. That the conflict occurs in the capital makes it all the more urgent, because Paul has finished in the east, at this point, and hopes to bring Rome and even Spain within purview of this ministry. Like the best military commanders, he takes a three-pronged approach.

First of all, he tells them insistently that he has longed to see them. This is an attempt to bridge the gap between himself and his readers. He has even included this desire in his prayers. 'For God, whom I serve with my spirit by announcing the gospel of his Son, is my witness that without ceasing I remember you always in my prayers, asking that by God's will I may somehow at last succeed in coming to you' (Rom 1:9-10). You can image the effect of hearing this: he makes the common relationship with God the foundation of his relationship with them.

Second, and this would take a great deal of unpacking, he argues with them in four great blocks. The first argument, chapters 1–4, is meant to destabilise the superiority of each group over the other.

> But now, apart from law, the righteousness of God has been disclosed, and is attested by the law and the prophets, the righteousness of God through faith in Jesus Christ for all who believe. For there is no distinction. (Rom 3:21-22)

> For there is no distinction between Jew and Greek; the same Lord is Lord of all and is generous to all who call on him. (Rom 10:12)

On the basis of actual moral achievement, they are on a very level playing field. The second argument, chapters 5–8, outlines in chronological order the gifts they share: salvation, faith, baptism, the help of the Holy Spirit, prayer, especially 'Abba Father', and unshakeable hope in Christ. The following question has been brewing all the time in the letter: 'If there is no difference between Jew and Gentile and if all are equally included under grace, what was or even is the point of being a Jew at all?' This very important question, which cannot detain us here, Paul deals with in chapters 9–11. Finally, he comes to practical instructions about how to live together, respect each other ('For as in one body we have many members, and not all the members have the same function, so we, who are many, are one body in Christ, and individually we are members one of another' [Rom 12:4-5]) and allow for reasonable differences over issues that are not essential to the faith. In 12:1–15:6 he offers the Roman Christians principles of discernment and a code of practice whereby the weak in faith should not be crushed by the overbearing freedom of the mature. It would, of course, have been possible to have written a much shorter letter, perhaps reducing it to the last section of hands-on comment. This, however, is not Paul's way of working. He presents in the fullest possible way why he gives the advice he gives. While this can be complex, at least he honours his hearers by giving them the means to understand where he is coming from. And he does not spare them. The letters *are* hard to read. It is assumed that the bearer had a role in explaining them. But at least he gives people all they need to understand the why of the recommendations behind the what. In that sense, while in Romans he talks about spirituality and even politics, he does not ignore the liberating effect of the intellectual grasp of the issues. And he hopes thereby to set them free from needless conflict and to enable them to discern the principles by which it is possible to distinguish the *diaphora* (Rom 12:6) from the *adiaphora*.

Third, at the end of the letter, when the listeners might begin to wonder what Paul knows of them anyway, he appends and comments on a rich list of characters, some of whom are fellow workers, all of whom he knows personally. The effect of this suddenly personal information is to lend authority to what he has just said because the extent of his familiarity suggests that he knows exactly what is going on in the Roman community. It is a subtle way of letting the Romans know just how detailed his knowledge is of them. In this letter, of course, there is no question of dealing with those he has left behind, but, by association, he links himself with the known grandees of the Roman house churches. This time, it is Paul the formidable intellect who is at work, not Paul the authoritarian nor Paul the personal bearer of Christ. And this time, it works like a dream. Because there is no real history of relationship, it is only our third example that seems relatively free of the effects of flaws in Paul's personality.

We have seen different aspects of the ministry of Paul: personal engagement, leadership challenges and his formidable intellect. We saw how he must by the very nature of his ministry embody the proclamation of God's unstinting love. This causes the Thessalonians to fail to understand the essential transience of his ministry among them. The Corinthians experience the opposite: they have moved on, but he thinks in the wrong way, and, in tension with the transience of his ministry, he reminds them of his irreplaceable position in their coming to the faith: they can have only one father. Yet, like any father, he has to let his children go. As secondary issues, the Thessalonians encounter his unwillingness to receive, just as the Corinthians encounter the emotional unevenness of Paul's personality. All that need for reconciliation was not caused by one side only. These problems reveal fundamental characteristics in Paul's personality, both enabling and inhibiting his effectiveness as a pastoral agent. *When I am weak, then I am strong.*

It also reveals something of the tensions, perhaps even contradictions, in his particular style: to be fully personally engaged and yet to be transient; to be enabling and claiming unique authority. These experiences are not limited to Paul of Tarsus. As we see, becoming a translucent agent of the Gospel, being a pastor who liberates and enables, was not something that Paul had learned once and for all. Instead, even long into his ministry, he still had to learn when to insist and when to let go. These experiences too are our own.

Chapter 11

ST PAUL AND THE LORD'S SUPPER

Being a Catholic Christian has (at least) four dimensions: the personal journey of faith, the experience of community belonging, the development of a reasonable faith and a strong commitment to justice, which includes care for the creation. It is unlikely that any of us would be able to inhabit all four dimensions equally at the one time; probably at different moments in life, one or other dimension comes to the fore. Nevertheless, a really integrated experience of discipleship would involve accessing more than one aspect of the faith and should really tend towards a full four-fold living of the Gospel. This four-fold grid can help us look at the experience of faith at two levels, as individuals and as a community. Traditional Irish Catholicism was strong on community belonging, expressed chiefly through going to Mass, and strong too on the commitment to justice, expressed through bodies such as the Vincent de Paul and donations to the missions and Third-World charities.

The habit of Mass-going is waning in our culture. There are many causes and reasons for this. It may help to observe that, in any case, attendance at Mass should be the weekly expression of something real and personal, the tip of the iceberg so to speak, rather than the only thing we ever do which is 'religious'. In reality, however, increasingly this is not the case: precisely because the real engagement with discipleship is much weaker, the celebration of that engagement at the weekly Eucharist is slowly losing its meaningfulness and therefore its hold.

Again, traditional Irish Catholicism was marked by social conformity but relatively poor in the understanding of the faith. The neglect of adult catechesis is now bearing unpleasant fruit: when you don't really know what is 'going on' at Mass, you don't really miss the experience when the habit of going wears off. I hope that doesn't sound too judgemental. St Jerome once said that the scriptures were like a sea in which an elephant can swim and a child can paddle. We may say something similar of the Eucharist. All the same, the Mass is a relatively sophisticated celebration of faith: it presumes a grasp of the Bible, the paschal mystery, discipleship and belonging to a community of faith, all finding symbolic expression in the sacrament of the Eucharist.

Without going down the route of the very tendentious, media references for example to transubstantiation show a real dearth of understanding of what is at stake. Furthermore, as the Mass really brings into the present the paschal mystery, the death and resurrection of Jesus, a meaningful participation must be based on a personal grasp of 'the paschal mystery'. We happen to live at a time between languages, so to speak. We used to have a very complete understanding of the cross and resurrection, an understanding proving inadequate for our time. Without a culturally resonant theology of Jesus' death and resurrection, the sacramental expression of the core events of Christianity loses something of *its* own resonance.

Add to the mix the common experience of the Eucharist and the extent of the current challenge becomes clear. Broadly speaking, in the larger parish churches, the Eucharist remains a rather individual experience. The community-creating potential of the celebration, while not totally absent, is much diminished. Probably the parish community is too large to feel much like a faith community. Belonging to the large parish needs to be mediated by a smaller belonging to some faith group – people who share prayer or bible study or some project. Such cells offer an adequate level of belonging, which can help us attain the larger belonging to the whole parish project as such.

At its best, the Eucharist is a sacrament *of disclosure*, disclosing the Risen Lord and the mutual belonging of all who take part. These two dimensions cannot properly be separated. The Lord's Supper was, in some respects, not without parallel in the ministry and life of Jesus. Jesus used meals ('open table-fellowship') to give people a concrete experience of his proclamation of the kingdom, that is, of the indiscriminate love of God. The Lord's Supper at the Last Supper brings to a climax the proclamation of God's reign, God's unconditional love for all without distinction. A Eucharist lacking a real community dimension simply misses the point: the disclosure of our mutual belonging in the love of God, as disciples of Christ.

Can we today find help in St Paul? At first glance it would seem not. After all, Paul rarely touches on the Eucharist. The occasional character of the letters of Paul may well account for the paucity of reference to the Eucharist. But even the Letter to the Romans, the most treatise-like of the documents, fails to mention the Lord's Supper. There, we might think, some mention of the Lord's Supper as a way of uniting believers in that conflicted community would not have been out of place. Perhaps the practice of the Lord's Supper in Rome was not contentious or problematic. The Eucharist does arise in the First Letter to the Corinthians, precisely because there was an issue about the practice in Corinth, an issue that in Paul's view undermined the sacrament and even emptied it of meaning. What was at stake and how did the apostle respond?

THE CRISIS IN CORINTH

Some recreation of the historical and community setting in Corinth is called for, already briefly undertaken in Chapter 10. Two passages from 1 Corinthians 11 can help us identify what was at stake:

> Now in the following instructions I do not commend you, because when you come together it is not for the better but for the worse. For, to begin with, when you come together as a church, I hear that there are divisions among you; and to some extent I believe it. Indeed, there have to be factions among you, for only so

will it become clear who among you are genuine. When you come together, it is not really to eat the Lord's supper. For when the time comes to eat, each of you goes ahead with your own supper, and one goes hungry and another becomes drunk. What! Do you not have homes to eat and drink in? Or do you show contempt for the church of God and humiliate those who have nothing? What should I say to you? Should I commend you? In this matter I do not commend you! (1 Cor 11:17-22)

So then, my brothers and sisters, when you come together to eat, wait for one another. If you are hungry, eat at home, so that when you come together, it will not be for your condemnation. (1 Cor 11:33-34)

The words are strong. In some way or other, the Lord's Supper is not really what it seems to be. It *seems* to be the Lord's Supper – Christians gather and do eat – but *in reality* it is not the Lord's Supper because the community remains divided. There is even effective exclusion of some.

THE CORINTHIAN CHRISTIANS

It helps to notice some features of the Corinthian experience. First of all, most of the Christians were from the poorer stratum of society, in terms of power, status, money and education. Paul admits as much when he writes, 'Consider your own call, brothers and sisters: not many of you were wise by human standards, not many were powerful, not many were of noble birth' (1 Cor 1:26-27). (Of course the fact that 'not many' were wise, powerful or noble means that at least *some* were.) Second, by necessity, the communities were based on house churches, that is, smaller social gatherings. That brought with it a tendency to clannishness and factions. Again, Paul admits to this when he writes: 'For it has been reported to me by Chloe's people that there are quarrels among you, my brothers and sisters. What I mean is that each of you says, "I belong to Paul", or "I belong to Apollos", or "I belong to Cephas", or "I belong to Christ"' (1 Cor 1:11-13). The same is found above in 1 Corinthians 11:17-22. Greco-Roman society as a whole was highly stratified and within that society the vast majority of the people had no influence or power or access to wealth or education. One of the features – one of the attractions really – of the Christian movement was the obliteration, within the community, of gender and socially constructed distinctions. Saint Paul himself notes this in Galatians: 'As many of you as were baptised into Christ have clothed yourselves with Christ. There is no longer Jew or Greek, there is no longer slave or free, there is no longer male and female; for all of you are one in Christ Jesus' (Gal 3:27-29). A more fully illustrated version of this sentiment may be found in the letter to the Colossians, where we read: 'In that renewal there is no longer Greek and Jew, circumcised and uncircumcised, barbarian, Scythian, slave and free; but Christ is all and in all!' (Col 3:11).

HOW THE CORINTHIANS CHURCHES 'CAME TOGETHER'

Scholars have wondered how and in what locations the very first generations of Christians gathered as communities (or 'came together', in Paul's technical language). From towns such as Ostia Antica, the port of ancient Rome, it is clear that the poor majority lived in blocks of flats called *insulae*. The spaces there would accommodate only quite small groups. The grander residences of a city such as Pompeii have given people some idea of how the very top echelons of society lived. Their houses are often termed 'villas' and in general these villas offered roughly the same facilities, such as an entrance (*atrium*), office (*tablinium*), dining room (*triclinium*) as well as other domestic spaces, such as bedrooms and a kitchen. Often there was a garden. From recent excavation at Ephesus, in modern-day Turkey, it is clear there was also a kind of middle-class – living comfortably, with frescoed rooms and mosaic floors. It would seem reasonable to assume that if the Christians came together in any number, the facilities of the better-off would need to have been utilised. Accordingly, it is often thought that the villas of richer Christians in Corinth were used to accommodate the larger 'coming together' of believers. Naturally, that was not without risks. In any society, even today, mixing people of different income levels and social backgrounds is complicated. All the more so in Greco-Roman society, which was so highly stratified. Pliny, in one of his letters, gives an amusing picture of such a scenario:

> I happened to be dining with a man, though no particular friend of his, whose elegant economy, as he called it, seemed to me a sort of stingy extravagance. The best dishes were set in front of himself and a select few, and the cheap scraps of food before the rest of the company. He had even put the wine into tiny little flasks, divided into three categories, not with the idea of giving his guests the opportunity to choose, but to make it impossible for them to refuse what they were given. One lot was intended for himself and for us, another for his lesser friends (all his friends are graded), and the third for his and our freedmen. (Letters 2:6)

'All his friends are graded' is very unkind and probably very accurate!

The meal practices of the day also help us to imagine what was happening at Corinth. In those days, an evening meal with invited guests unfolded in two parts. The first part was the meal, the *deipnon*, served in the *triclinium*. The second part was a drinks party, technically a *symposium*, at which there might be entertainment or more serious discussions of philosophy, politics and the like, as well as plenty of alcohol. Greco-Roman dinners were small. The ideal numbers was proverbially no fewer than the graces (three) and no more than the muses (nine). In the case of nine guests, for example, the important guests would recline beside the host, then the next three on the nearest side, and furthest away the three least important guests. They would even recline in order of importance, friend number one right beside the host and so on down to the unlucky last one. On a very practical note, it has been calculated that on average the typically sized villa of the Greco-Roman world would comfortably hold only about fifty people. Such calculations have a wide margin of error, but it permits us to imagine, on the basis of the named factions and allowing for others, that the Corinthian community was made up of about 250 to 400 adherents. It is striking to remember that when Paul wrote 'to the Corinthians', it was not at all to the estimated 80–100,000 inhabitants of the city in his day, but rather to the very few, probably less than 500, who happened to be followers of Christ. Finally, accommodating around fifty would have meant using all the public spaces of the house – the *triclinium*, the *atrium* and the garden for example. That in itself would have inhibited the sense of community at any coming-together.

To go back to the community meetings, the risk at the gatherings of any particular house church is that these deeply embedded social mores of the relatively well-off and the rich would reassert themselves and the poor would be made to feel unwelcome. This would be very much contrary to the Christian vision as enunciated by St Paul.

THE SUPPER AND THE LORD'S SUPPER

As is clear from 1 Corinthians, the Lord's Supper at this time still took place in the course of the ordinary supper, or evening meal, of the day. Looking back from current liturgical practice, with fasting and so forth, this can be a surprise. However, given Jesus' practice of table-fellowship and the fact that the first Lord's Supper took place during a meal at Passover time, it is not really all that surprising.

In light of all that, we can understand what was happening at the coming together of the Church, looking at a passage mentioned at the start of this chapter:

> When you come together, it is not really to eat the
> Lord's supper. For when the time comes to eat, *each*

of you goes ahead with your own supper, and one goes hungry and another becomes drunk. What! Do you not have homes to eat and drink in? Or do you show contempt for the church of God and humiliate those who have nothing? (1 Cor 11:20-22; emphasis added)

Some Corinthians, for whatever reason, cannot make the start of the Lord's Supper, and when they do arrive, the food is gone and the early birds have moved on to the drinks party. Most likely, it is the slaves who cannot keep appointments and the wealthy do not wait for them. The practical advice is *very* practical:

So then, my brothers and sisters, when you come together to eat, *wait for one another.* If you are hungry, eat at home, so that when you come together, it will not be for your condemnation. (1 Cor 11:33-34; emphasis added)

TEACHING ON THE LORD'S SUPPER

Within his general response to this crisis in Corinth, Paul presents his positive teaching about the supper in two stages. The first stage is a reminder of the tradition:

For I received from the Lord what I also handed on to you, that the Lord Jesus on the night when he was betrayed took a loaf of bread, and when he had given thanks, he broke it and said, 'This is my body that is for you. Do this in remembrance of me'. In the same way he took the cup also, after supper, saying, 'This cup is the new covenant in my blood. Do this, as often as you drink it, in remembrance of me'. For as often as you eat this bread and drink the cup, you proclaim the Lord's death until he comes. (1 Cor 11:23-26)

The application of the tradition is revealing.

> Whoever, therefore, eats the bread or drinks the cup of the Lord in an unworthy manner will be answerable for the body and blood of the Lord. Examine yourselves, and only then eat of the bread and drink of the cup. For all who eat and drink without discerning the body, eat and drink judgement against themselves. For this reason many of you are weak and ill, and some have died. But if we judged ourselves, we would not be judged. But when we are judged by the Lord, we are disciplined so that we may not be condemned along with the world. (1 Cor 11:27-32)

The first and second sentences really belong together. There can be 'unworthiness' and the Corinthians are instructed to examine themselves. The third sentence is a key: 'For all who eat and drink without discerning the body, eat and drink judgement against themselves.' A devotional tradition would see here a moral unworthiness or a failure to believe in the Real Presence. These explanations seem to me to be anachronistic. The presenting issue is the failure to discern the *social* body of Christ, that is, contempt for the Church of God and humiliation of those who have nothing. The real issue is that the community is not really a community and the Lord's Supper is not really the Lord's Supper, as Paul says. The body of Christ is being violated but it is the social body of Christ. Two texts seem to confirm this understanding.

> The cup of blessing that we bless, is it not a sharing in the blood of Christ? The bread that we break, is it not a sharing in the body of Christ? Because there is one bread, we who are many are one body, for we all partake of the one bread. (1 Cor 10:16-17)

> For just as the body is one and has many members,
> and all the members of the body, though many, are
> one body, so it is with Christ. For in the one Spirit we
> were all baptised into one body – Jews or Greeks,
> slaves or free – and we were all made to drink of one
> Spirit. (1 Cor 12:12-13)

This reflects the understanding of Eucharist proposed at the start: the sacrament is a sacrament of *disclosure*, that is, disclosure in the interpersonal sense. In the words over the bread, the risen Lord discloses himself to the gathered believers. At the same time, the believers are disclosed as brothers and sisters to each other. The very function of the Eucharist is the building up of the body of the Christ and the Mass is very properly called the sacrament of unity. It declares and creates the communion of believers in Christ. In an ecclesiastical setting where the community dimension is real and alive, then the sacrament is at its most effective. Where the communion dimension is diminished or even absent, then a constitutive element of the sacrament is missing. Saint Paul would go even further: 'When you come together, it is not really to eat the Lord's supper' (1 Cor 11:19-21). We might not like to express it so strongly because no Eucharist is ever really perfect in that sense. Nevertheless, to feel the tension is salutary.

Chapter 12

WOMEN IN THE PAULINE ASSEMBLIES

There is no doubt that there are difficult texts in the New Testament on the place of women in the Church and in the world. In particular, texts associated with St Paul cause pain and offence to women and to men. An example would be 1 Timothy 2:8-15, which reads:

> I desire, then, that in every place the men should pray, lifting up holy hands without anger or argument; also that the women should dress themselves modestly and decently in suitable clothing, not with their hair braided, or with gold, pearls, or expensive clothes, but with good works, as is proper for women who profess reverence for God. Let a woman learn in silence with full submission. I permit no woman to teach or to have authority over a man; she is to keep silent. For Adam was formed first, then Eve; and Adam was not deceived, but the woman was deceived and became a transgressor. Yet she will be saved through childbearing, provided they continue in faith and love and holiness, with modesty. (1 Tim 2:8-15; cf. also Ephesians 5:22-31; Colossians 3:18-25; 1 Timothy 5:1-2; 6:1-2; Titus 2:1-10; 3:1.)

In dealing with St Paul's teachings about women, it is essential to establish first of all which texts may be attributed to him. As noted previously, very many scholars would hold that 1 and 2 Timothy and Titus cannot be attributed to the apostle himself. They are in the Pauline tradition, but reflect the concerns and settings of the next generation of the Church, with a much more structured ministry. It may seem strange to us, but at the time, writing in the name of some established figure was not at all unusual. Not quite so many scholars but still perhaps a majority would hold that Ephesians and Colossians are also not by the same hand that wrote the genuine letters. This is a complex issue. The deciding factor for me is the change in theological focus and the quite different manner of writing (not just the vocabulary). Hebrews, does not count at all because its world of reference is just so distinct. Two Thessalonians has a disputed relationship with 1 Thessalonians. In summary, when reconstructing the teaching about women in the letters of St Paul, we are limited to seven documents, that is, Romans, 1 and 2 Corinthians, Galatians, Philippians, 1 Thessalonians and Philemon. In these documents only, what does the apostle say?

The foundational statement about the sexes is found in the mighty letter to the Galatians, where Paul writes:

> As many of you as were baptised into Christ have clothed yourselves with Christ. There is no longer Jew or Greek, there is no longer slave or free, there is no longer male and female; for all of you are one in Christ Jesus. And if you belong to Christ, then you are Abraham's offspring, heirs according to the promise. (Gal 3:27-29)

This radical equality remains his fundamental attitude, an attitude in dynamic continuity with the practice and teaching of Jesus himself. It is, to say the least, in some tension with 1 Timothy 2:8-15. What about Paul's application of his principles?

At a quite personal level, Paul teaches the sexual equality of men and women. The key text here is 1 Corinthians 7:

> Now concerning the matters about which you wrote: 'It is well for a man not to touch a woman.' But because of cases of sexual immorality, each man should have his own wife and each woman her own husband. The

husband should give to his wife her conjugal rights, and likewise the wife to her husband. For the wife does not have authority over her own body, but the husband does; likewise the husband does not have authority over his own body, but the wife does. Do not deprive one another except perhaps by agreement for a set time, to devote yourselves to prayer, and then come together again, so that Satan may not tempt you because of your lack of self-control. This I say by way of concession, not of command. I wish that all were as I myself am. But each has a particular gift from God, one having one kind and another a different kind. (1 Cor 7:1-7)

The first thing to notice is that ancient Greek and Latin did not use inverted commas. It was not always obvious that at the start of this passage Paul is not giving his own opinion, but rather quoting one of the factions in Corinth. That faction seems to think that sex is best avoided. Paul clearly disagrees with that, suggesting mutually agreed abstinence for brief periods only. In this he remains a regular Jew, with a healthy acceptance of sexuality as God's gift. He does not suffer from the later Christian preoccupation with sexuality, perhaps under the influence of Greek philosophy and the monastic movement. In 1 Corinthians, he quotes slogans from the factions in Corinth and the opening opinion is one such slogan.

There is, however, an apparent echo of 1 Timothy 2:8-15 in 1 Corinthians 14. The text reads as follows (this time I leave in the verse references for convenience):

[29]Let two or three prophets speak, and let the others weigh what is said. [30]If a revelation is made to someone else sitting nearby, let the first person be silent. [31]For you can all prophesy one by one, so that all may learn and all be encouraged. [32]And the spirits of prophets are subject to the prophets, [33]for God is a God not of

disorder but of peace. (As in all the churches of the saints, [34]women should be silent in the churches. For they are not permitted to speak, but should be subordinate, as the law also says. [35]If there is anything they desire to know, let them ask their husbands at home. For it is shameful for a woman to speak in church. [36]Or did the word of God originate with you? Or are you the only ones it has reached?) [37]Anyone who claims to be a prophet, or to have spiritual powers, must acknowledge that what I am writing to you is a command of the Lord. [38]Anyone who does not recognise this is not to be recognised.

This is the *New Revised Standard Version*. Just as ancient Greek did not use inverted commas, neither did it use parentheses. Yet the translation has part of the text in parentheses. This indicates that the text in question may not be part of the original letter. Scholars give three reasons for this. First of all, if read from v.33 to v.37, the text reads perfectly smoothly. Paul is not dealing with women in 1 Corinthians 14 but with the appropriate use of the spiritual gifts in the Christian assembly. Second, it contradicts his principle that there is no distinction in Christ between male and female. Third and most revealingly, it contradicts his practice of having women as fellow workers, deacons and even in one case an apostle. The key text here is Romans 16 to which we now turn (again the verse numbers are retained within the text for convenience; emphasis added).

[1]I commend to you our sister *Phoebe*, a *deacon* of the church at Cenchreae, [2]so that you may welcome her in the Lord as is fitting for the saints, and help her in whatever she may require from you, for she has been a *benefactor* of many and of myself as well.

[3]Greet *Prisca and Aquila*, who *work* with me in Christ Jesus, [4]and who risked their necks for my life, to whom

not only I give thanks, but also all the churches of the Gentiles. [5]Greet also the church in their house. Greet my beloved Epaenetus, who was the first convert in Asia for Christ. [6]Greet *Mary*, who has *worked* very hard among you. [7]Greet Andronicus and *Junia*, my relatives who were in prison with me; *they are prominent among the apostles*, and they were in Christ before I was. [8]Greet Ampliatus, my beloved in the Lord. [9]Greet Urbanus, our co-worker in Christ, and my beloved Stachys. [10]Greet Apelles, who is approved in Christ. Greet those who belong to the family of Aristobulus. [11]Greet my relative Herodion. Greet those in the Lord who belong to the family of Narcissus. [12]Greet those *workers* in the Lord, *Tryphaena* and *Tryphosa*. Greet the beloved *Persis*, who has *worked* hard in the Lord.

The unsuspecting reader may not notice that the terms 'worked' or 'worker' are technical terms for evangelisers. Among those who 'worked hard', Paul mentioned five women: Prisca (v.3), Mary (v.6), Tryphaena, Tyrphosa and Persis (v.12). We know little about these figures (with the exception of Prisca), but they are women who preached and taught the Gospel. At the start of the passage, Paul mentions Phoebe (v.1), deacon of the Church at Cenchreae, near Corinth. 'Deacon' at this stage did not bear the meaning of 'ordained deacon' but it does mean the person in charge, with responsibility for the Church. Finally, Junia (v.7), an actual relative of Paul, is mentioned as 'prominent among the apostles', no less. It just is not possible for women to take on the roles of evangelist, deacon and apostle without being able to speak at the assembly! This is the strongest argument for thinking that the inserted passage in 1 Corinthians 14 must be just that, an insertion, an interpolation. It may very well have come from the time when 1 Timothy was penned and inserted here to draw on the support of Paul for a later, much more conservative view of women in the Christian movement.

The other important text to comment on is found in 1
Corinthians 11, a difficult text to handle.

> But I want you to understand that Christ is the head of
> every man, and the husband is the head of his wife, and
> God is the head of Christ. Any man who prays or
> prophesies with something on his head disgraces his
> head, but any woman who prays or prophesies with her
> head unveiled disgraces her head – it is one and the
> same thing as having her head shaved. For if a woman
> will not veil herself, then she should cut off her hair; but
> if it is disgraceful for a woman to have her hair cut off or
> to be shaved, she should wear a veil. For a man ought
> not to have his head veiled, since he is the image and
> reflection of God; but woman is the reflection of man.
> Indeed, man was not made from woman, but woman
> from man. Neither was man created for the sake of
> woman, but woman for the sake of man. For this reason
> a woman ought to have a symbol of authority on her
> head, because of the angels. Nevertheless, in the Lord
> woman is not independent of man or man independent
> of woman. For just as woman came from man, so man
> comes through woman; but all things come from God.
> Judge for yourselves: is it proper for a woman to pray
> to God with her head unveiled? Does not nature itself
> teach you that if a man wears long hair, it is degrading
> to him, but if a woman has long hair, it is her glory? For
> her hair is given to her for a covering. But if anyone is
> disposed to be contentious – we have no such custom,
> nor do the churches of God. (1 Cor 11:3-16)

First of all, we may observe that the practice being encouraged here
applies equally to men and to women. There is an interesting
translation problem here. The words 'with his head covered' translate
an idiom in Greek meaning 'having down on the head', where the word

'down' is an adverb: having something *downwards* on his head. It could mean having his hair hanging down. The words 'with her head unveiled' translates another expression in Greek which means literally 'having down(wards) on the head'. Again, it could mean having your hair literally down or worn long. The problem may not be the head-covering at all but hairstyles. This reading may seem threatened by vv.14-16: 'Does not nature itself teach you that if a man wears long hair, it is degrading to him, but if a woman has long hair, it is her glory? For her hair is given to her for a covering' (1 Cor 11:14-16) This text confirms that in the case of men, the issue is the length of hair. For women, the word 'covering' in v.16 means literally 'in a knot'. It is known from illustrations on Greek vases and statuary that men and women who were homosexual wore their hair down, that is, long, while heterosexual men wore their hair short, and heterosexual women, tied up into a bun on top of the head. Paul's anxiety here has to do with God's ordering of the sexes at creation. He remains a faithful Jew, deeply distressed at the blurring of such distinctions apparent and acceptable in Gentile culture. The argument, therefore, is very specific to Greco-Roman culture. Paul confirms his case by a somewhat specious argument from hierarchy, based on a reading of Genesis 2, and then closes in the tone of someone who wants to insist but has run out of reasonable argument: 'But if anyone is disposed to be contentious – we have no such custom, nor do the churches of God' (1 Cor 11:16). With current issues of sexuality very much contended in our culture, it may not help that a head-covering issue has been transformed into a homosexual one, but at least it promotes a more accurate contextual reading of the passage.

In summary, Paul teaches the equality of the sexes in principle (Galatians 3). Consistent with that are his opinions about sex (1 Corinthians 7) and ministry (Romans 16). He wavers somewhat on the domestic front, holding to a hierarchy descending from God through Christ, man and eventually woman (1 Corinthians 11). The blurring of the sexual distinctions – not the same at all as equality – is the issue there. The important thing for us today is to remember that Paul had no problem with women in ministry, as evangelisers, as deacons (that is, in charge of a church) and as apostles. Clearly, such women by virtue of their calling and role were entitled to speak in the assembly. This more radical view of the first generation was abandoned as the Church of the second generation settled down and conformed to society's expectations. It is a warning of some kind and there may even be something here for us to learn today.

Chapter 13

WHERE TO FROM HERE?[1]

INTRODUCTION

Assessing the damage after an earthquake is a harrowing experience: there is the loss of life, the continued threat of aftershocks and, eventually, the daunting task of rebuilding. The Report of the Commission of Investigation in the Catholic Archdiocese of Dublin has had a similarly harrowing impact. First and foremost, the 'loss of life', that is the stolen childhoods of so many in our care, is and remains the immediate and most lasting harm done. The aftershocks continue: seemingly ongoing, ever more vile disclosures, bishops in jeopardy, and even the gospel itself undermined by rank failures in justice and morality. The aftershocks will be with us for the foreseeable future. It is right, even 'good' – if such a word can be used – that all this should come out into the open. Protection and concealment did unspeakable harm, first of all to the victims, and now, as we see, not only to the Church but to the Gospel project.

There are many dimensions to this earthquake: spiritual, pastoral, psychological, social, financial, legal and so forth. Each of these has it's own validity. There are also, it seems to me, properly *theological* questions which understandably receive less attention in the critical moment as the ground gives way beneath us. To some, it will even seem indecent haste to address these questions so soon. One thing, however, is sure: we are all asking these questions. What does all this say about the Church, past and present, and where do we go into the future? Somehow, we have to try to hold the pain and our hope together.

1. An earlier version of this chapter appeared in the January issue of *Doctrine and Life*, 2010.

Among the resources we turn to is the Bible and, in particular, to the apostle Paul. Saint Paul can help us today because from his pen we have direct knowledge of the communities he worked for, we have the benefit of his analysis of what can go wrong in 'Church' and, perhaps, we can use him to begin to look at the rebuilding process.

In this short reflection, I would like to look at insights from St Paul so as to name what went wrong and to begin to talk about where to go from here: (1) boasting and (2) faith, (3) conversion and (4) power.

(1) Boasting[2]

The Letter to the Romans was written to a Church divided along ethnic lines between Jews and Gentiles. The Jews had been the founding and guiding influence until the expulsion of Christian Jews under Claudius as reported in Acts 18:2 and in some other secular documents of the period. In the subsequent vacuum, the Roman (Gentile) Christians evolved a style of being Christian that differed considerably: they dropped the markers of Jewish identity (circumcision, dietary laws, Sabbath observance) and were not concerned about meat sacrificed to idols. When the expulsion of the 'Jews' – i.e. those few Jewish *Christians* causing trouble – was relaxed and it was possible for them to return, a conflict broke out between Christians of Gentile origin and Christians of Jewish origin, in the very capital itself. Previously dominant, the Christian Jews hoped to reclaim their previous entitlement.

This is the context into which Paul wrote. The issue mattered greatly to him because his core vision was the breaking down of the wall between Jew and Gentile, in the light of Jesus' crucifixion and resurrection.[3]

Paul regarded the claims of each side as 'boasting'. It would have been possible for the Gentiles to have claimed a more mature insight

2. Boasting, as verb and as noun, can be found in: Rom 2:17, 23; 4:2; 5:2–3, 11; 1 Cor 1:29, 31; 3:21; 4:7; 5:6; 9:15–16; 13:3; 2 Cor 1:14; 5:12; 7:14; 9:2–3; 10:8, 13, 15–17; 11:12, 16, 18, 30; 12:1, 5–6, 9; Gal 6:4, 13–14; Phil 1:26; 2:16; 3:3.
3. For he is our peace; in his flesh he has made both groups into one and has broken down the dividing wall, that is, the hostility between us (Eph 2:14).

into following Christ, perhaps with something like the words of Galatians ringing in their ears, 'for freedom Christ has set us free'. Conversely, it would also have been possible for the Jews to have claimed a more faithful insight into following the Messiah, perhaps with something resembling the words of Romans ringing in their ears, 'to them (i.e. *to us*) belong the adoption, the glory, the covenants, the giving of the law, the worship, and the promises; to them belong the patriarchs, and from them, according to the flesh, comes the Messiah'. In any case, 'boasting' was the result, with each side regarding the others as inferior and themselves as superior.[4]

Saint Paul's approach in Romans 1–4 is powerful and risky. He destabilises *both* sides by exposing past and present moral failure, thus removing grounds for boasting. In effect, he insults them, beginning with the Gentile Christians (Rom 1:18-32) and tricks the Jewish Christians into judging their Gentile brothers and sisters,[5] perhaps triggering an involuntary sentiment along the lines of 'at last, one of our own speaking with authority, putting these Gentiles in their place'. He then turns on the Jewish Christians and in a sharp paragraph he excoriates them:

> But if you call yourself a Jew and rely on the law and boast of your relation to God and know his will and determine what is best because you are instructed in the law, and if you are sure that you are a guide to the blind, a light to those who are in darkness, a corrector of the foolish, a teacher of children, having in the law the embodiment of knowledge and truth, you, then, that teach others, will you not teach yourself? While you preach against stealing, do you steal? You that forbid adultery, do you commit adultery? You that abhor idols,

4. A phenomenon not unknown today.
5. Therefore you have no excuse, whoever you are, when you judge others; for in passing judgment on another you condemn yourself, because you, the judge, are doing the very same things (Rom 2:1).

do you rob temples? You that boast in the law, do you
dishonour God by breaking the law? For, as it is written,
'The name of God is blasphemed among the Gentiles
because of you.' (Rom 2:17-24)

This devastating passage could be brought up to date with the
following adjustments:

But if you call yourself a Catholic and rely on the
institution and boast of your relation to God and know
his will and determine what is best because you are
instructed in the doctrine, and if you are sure that you
are a guide to the blind, a light to those who are in
darkness, a corrector of the foolish, a teacher of
children, having in the Church the embodiment of
knowledge and truth, you, then, that teach others, will
you not teach yourself? While you preach against abuse,
do you abuse? You that forbid adultery, do you commit
adultery? You that abhor injustice, do you practice
injustice? You that boast in the Gospel, do you
dishonour God by breaking the Gospel? For, as it is
written, 'The name of God is blasphemed among non-
believers because of you.'

There are three elements in this passage from Paul: attitudes, failures
and consequences. There are parallels between the *attitudes* of the
Roman Christian Jews and the Roman Catholic Church. Chiefly, it
amounts to an attitude of great superiority (over against other
Churches in particular),[6] a distorted confidence in 'being Catholic' as
sufficient in itself and a deafness to the core of the Gospel as applying
to ourselves. Saint Paul would package it all as 'boasting', that is,
standing on status, on a name, on a tradition. He might even put to
us the two questions he puts to the Jewish Christians: Is there any

6.   For example, in *Dominus Jesus*.

advantage in being a Catholic? *Much, in every way.*[7] Are we any better off? *No, not at all.*[8]

The Church, as an institution, has held up demanding ideals – especially in morality and sexual morality in particular – while *failing* itself, at least in some representatives, to heed its own teaching. The protection of minors from continued threat and harm was simply a question of justice. The words of Paul are penetrating, 'you, then, that teach others, will you not teach yourself?' His purpose at this point in Romans is to produce grief – not just any kind of distress but 'godly grief'. As he says himself elsewhere 'godly grief produces a repentance that leads to salvation and brings no regret, but worldly grief produces death.' (2 Cor 7:9-11) As for the *consequences*: 'The name of God is blasphemed among the Gentiles because of you.' Or more simply, 'The name of God is blasphemed because of you.' In a word, the gospel project has been materially undermined – I avoid saying fatally wounded – because of what happened. Bringing the Good News itself into disrepute constitutes a trenchant critique, which goes to the heart of the *raison d'être* of the Church.

(2) Faith[9]

In the same Romans 1–4, Paul not only diagnoses moral failure, undermines 'boasting' and names the consequences, he also proposes a way out, a solution. Going back to the biblical example of Abraham but applying it to Christ, he writes:

7. Then what advantage has the Jew? Or what is the value of circumcision? Much, in every way. For in the first place the Jews were entrusted with the oracles of God (Rom 3:1-2).
8. What then? Are we any better off? No, not at all; for we have already charged that all, both Jews and Greeks, are under the power of sin (Rom 3:9).
9. Paul's reflections on faith are rich and varied: Rom 1:5, 8, 12, 16–17; 3:2–3, 22, 25–28, 30–31; 4:3, 5, 9, 11–14, 16–20, 24; 5:1–2; 6:8; 9:30, 32–33; 10:4, 6, 8–11, 14, 16–17; 11:20; 12:3, 6; 13:11; 14:1–2, 22–23; 15:13; 16:26; 1 Cor 1:9, 21; 2:5; 3:5; 4:2, 17; 7:25; 9:17; 10:13; 11:18; 12:9; 13:2, 7, 13; 14:22; 15:2, 11, 14, 17; 16:13; 2 Cor 1:18, 24; 4:13; 5:7; 6:15; 8:7; 10:15; 13:5; Gal 1:23; 2:7, 16, 20; 3:2, 5–9, 11–12, 14, 22–26; 5:5–6, 22; 6:10; Phil 1:25, 27, 29; 2:17; 3:9; 1 Thess 1:3, 7–8; 2:4, 10, 13; 3:2, 5–7, 10; 4:14; 5:8, 24; Phlm 5–6.

But now, apart from law, the righteousness of God has been disclosed, and is attested by the law and the prophets, the righteousness of God through the *fidelity of Jesus Christ* for all who believe. For there is no distinction, since all have sinned and fall short of the glory of God; they are now justified by his grace as a gift, through the redemption that is in Christ Jesus, whom God put forward as a *mercy seat* by his blood, effective *through his* (i.e. Jesus') *fidelity*. He did this to show his righteousness, because in his divine forbearance he had passed over the sins previously committed; it was to prove at the present time that he himself is righteous and that he justifies the one *who lives from the fidelity of Jesus* (Rom 3:21-26 NRSV adjusted).

The reader will notice that the translation offered just now is an adjustment of the NRSV. There is a large scholarly discussion of the expression 'faith in/of Jesus', because the Greek can mean *either* the believer's faith in Jesus *or* the fidelity which Jesus himself had.[10] The usual translation, found in virtually all popular Bibles, doesn't quite make sense as it stands and, it seems to me, those who translate this (and other passages) as the *fidelity of Christ* are more accurate.

The consequences of this choice of translation are substantial. Paul is *not* saying the believer is saved by the believer's *own* faith. Rather, Paul is saying the believer is 'justified', that is put in 'right relationship' with God, by means of the fidelity/faith of Jesus. Paul has in mind a kind of Christ-mysticism: we can relate to God by means of Jesus' *own* faith in and fidelity towards God. Faith is no longer a matter of just believing doctrines. Faith is no longer even 'my' faith in God and in Christ. Faith is rather the offer of a bridge relationship put in place by God in Christ so that the faith 'alone' by which I am saved is that very relationship which Christ had/has with the Father. This is a deeply personalised vision of faith, on the

10. The ambiguous expression – in Greek *pistis tou Christou* – can be found in Rom 3:22; Gal 2:16; 3:22, 24, 26; Phil 3:9. For many scholars, the reading offered above is essential for Romans and Philippians. It also illuminates – and radically changes – the reading of Galatians.

strength of which it is possible finally to live as God would have us live. In Paul's vision, the impasse of moral failure – deeply embedded in human nature before and after the Law – can actually be overcome by God's offer of an extraordinary relationship, a love 'stronger than death'. In our Church today we have experienced a systemic impasse of moral failure. This is more than an administrative issue and touches the heart of being a disciple in the first place. How can we access this new relationship, this transformed way of being?

(3) Conversion

The raw self-examination of Church right now must take conversion in both of its dimensions. Firstly, conversion means repentance, a looking back and a heartfelt acknowledgement of wrongdoing and a taking of responsibility.[11] There can be no doubt that we are in for a long period of repentance as a community of faith. As Jeremiah put it in the context of Babylonian exile, 'build houses and live in them', meaning this is not going to be short, so inhabit the experience (Jer 29:4-7). At the same time, our hope is that this time of grief will be a time of godly grief (2 Cor 7:9-11). It will be merely worldly grief if treated simply as a 'management' problem, as an institutional challenge to get it right in terms of the media etc. In contrast to such merely human 'regret', godly grief leads to Christ.

The Greek word repentance – *metanoia* – means significantly more than regret or repentance. *Metanoia* means a new mind, an entirely new way of looking at reality. Paul only rarely uses this gospel term but the reality is fully present in his letters. The preferred expression in Paul for the changed reality of the believer is 'being in Christ'.[12] He puts it succinctly in Philippians: *Let the same mind be in*

---

11. It is used in this largely moral sense by Paul in Rom 2:4; 2 Cor 7:9-10; 12:21.
12. The texts are many: Rom 3:24; 6:11, 23; 8:1-2, 39-9:1; 12:5; 15:17; 16:3, 7, 9-10; 1 Cor 1:2, 4, 30; 3:1; 4:10, 15, 17; 15:18-19, 22, 31; 16:24; 2 Cor 2:10, 14, 17; 3:14; 5:17, 19; 12:2, 19; Gal 1:6, 22; 2:4, 17, 20; 3:14, 26, 28; 5:6; Phil 1:1, 8, 13, 26; 2:1, 5; 3:3, 14; 4:7, 19, 21; 1 Thess 2:14; 4:16; 5:18; Phlm 8, 20, 23.

you that was in Christ Jesus (Phil 2:5).[13] This is an individual 'conversion' and also a community challenge.

Paul's own entry into being 'in Christ' was a fruit of his encounter with the risen Jesus (1 Cor 15:8; Gal 1:13-17). The nature of that encounter and its subsequent interpretation by Paul can be grasped only if we ask *why* Paul persecuted the Christians. Paul persecuted the early Church because he opposed, on theological grounds, the claim that Jesus, a crucified man, was raised from death and could be acclaimed as messiah and Lord. Paul *knew* this to be false on account of the word of God: *anyone hung on a tree is under God's curse* (Deut 21:23). The encounter with the risen Jesus meant immediately that Paul now knew God was in Christ reconciling the world to himself (2 Cor 5:19). Paul's coming to faith was indistinguishable from his calling as an apostle. From now on his life, his very self would be the proclamation of what God had done in Christ.[14] He himself, crucified with Christ, would show in himself what he had discovered in Christ.[15] This was the only way to be a credible bearer of the Good News in the culture of the time – and it remains today the only way.

(4) Power

Being 'in Christ', being converted to use the Gospel term, has consequences for leadership and for the exercise of power. Under the headings of weakness and strength, Paul discusses the thorny topic of power. His encounter with the risen Lord caused him to understand the cross in a completely new light: *God's foolishness is wiser than*

---

13. Compare: Do not be conformed to this world, but be transformed by the renewing of your minds, so that you may discern what is the will of God – what is good and acceptable and perfect (Rom 12:2).
14. So deeply do we care for you that we are determined to share with you not only the gospel of God but also our own selves, because you have become very dear to us (1 Thess 2:8).
15. I have been crucified with Christ; and it is no longer I who live, but it is Christ who lives in me. And the life I now live in the flesh I live by the fidelity of the Son of God, who loved me and gave himself for me (Gal 2:19-21).

human wisdom, and God's weakness is stronger than human strength (1 Cor 1:25). God's most 'powerful' way of being God was through the weakness of the cross, in compassionate, loving solidarity. Already from Mark's Gospel we know the consequences of having a crucified messiah for discipleship and leadership:

> So Jesus called them and said to them, 'You know that among the Gentiles those whom they recognise as their rulers lord it over them, and their great ones are tyrants over them. But it is not so among you; but whoever wishes to become great among you must be your servant, and whoever wishes to be first among you must be slave of all. For the Son of Man came not to be served but to serve, and to give his life a ransom for many.' (Mark 10:42-45)

Paul has exactly the same idea. In himself, as an apostle, he knows Christ and he displays Christ, not by aping worldly power, but by making his own the weakness of Christ: *for whenever I am weak, then I am strong* (2 Cor 12:10). This part of his experience of Christ, his identity as an apostle[16] and, even we may use the term, his spirituality.[17]

---

16. When I came to you, brothers and sisters, I did not come proclaiming the mystery of God to you in lofty words or wisdom. For I decided to know nothing among you except Jesus Christ, and him crucified. And I came to you in weakness and in fear and in much trembling. My speech and my proclamation were not with plausible words of wisdom, but with a demonstration of the Spirit and of power, so that your faith might rest not on human wisdom but on the power of God (1 Cor 2:1-5).
17. I want you to know, beloved that what has happened to me has actually helped to spread the gospel, so that it has become known throughout the whole imperial guard and to everyone else that my imprisonment is for Christ; and most of the brothers and sisters, having been made confident in the Lord by my imprisonment, dare to speak the word with greater boldness and without fear (Phil 1:12-14).

Into old age, Paul was still engaged with the Gospel. In a moving passage in what might be his last letter, the aged Paul wrote:

> I want to know Christ and the power of his resurrection and the sharing of his sufferings by becoming like him in his death, if somehow I may attain the resurrection from the dead. Not that I have already obtained this or have already reached the goal; but I press on to make it my own, because Christ Jesus has made me his own. Beloved, I do not consider that I have made it my own; but this one thing I do: forgetting what lies behind and straining forward to what lies ahead, I press on toward the goal for the prize of the heavenly call of God in Christ Jesus. (Phil 3:10-15)

But most movingly of all, he speaks of himself as crucified with Christ: *I have been crucified with Christ; and it is no longer I who live, but it is Christ who lives in me* (Gal 2:19-20). Paul is saying that his encounter with Christ has penetrated so deeply into his being, that he wants nothing other than to be Christ to those whom he serves. Just as Christ, on the cross, embraced all without distinction so that there is no longer Jew nor Greek, slave nor free, Paul wishes to be a sacrament of that same embrace. This is his 'spirituality' of apostleship and his claim to authority rests on being 'in Christ'.

In our time we seek, we need, religious leaders with the weakness and the strength of Paul, who will speak to us not officially or ecclesiastically, that is, *from on high*, but *from within*, whose authority does not come finally from position or even from law but from *the only teacher*.[18] Do we want leadership of any other kind? Has the other kind of 'service' been of service to us? Just as the regeneration of Church

---

18. But you are not to be called rabbi, for you have one teacher, and you are all students. And call no one your father on earth, for you have one Father – the one in heaven. Nor are you to be called instructors, for you have one instructor, the Messiah. The greatest among you will be your servant (Mt 23:8-12).

can have no genesis apart from the faith and fidelity of Christ, likewise the regeneration of Christian leadership can have no genesis apart from the *magister*, Christ himself, who came not to be served but to serve, modelling the only valid Christian *magisterium*. This is really a conversion because the default position is 'making your authority felt', the all-too-human model of lording it over others. In practice, we have Church structures mirroring clearly the values and trappings of the earthly kingdom and with equal clarity obscuring the values of the Kingdom of God. In theory, that part of the Church most open to reform is its structures. In reality, it is the least open to revision, alas, because the central administration is always impervious, always imperious. At least the local Church is learning vulnerability and so coming closer to true discipleship and apostleship.

CONCLUSION

If the Church as a community of believers is to become again a bearer of the Good News in our culture, we must begin by abandoning boasting of any kind. At the centre must stand the faith/fidelity of Christ by means of which we may relate to God and live the tremendous demands of the Gospel. Of course we will evolve catechetical programmes; of course we will try to make liturgy better; of course there will be new ways of understanding the Bible and the tradition. But none of this will be of more than apparent significance unless the core is in place: God's gift of relationship, offered through the faith of Christ, lived through the faith of believers. That transformation of self and of community must then penetrate into leadership, to leadership of true discipleship, without the trappings and attitudes of the worldly *imperium*. To put it briefly, the over-centralised and self-regarding bureaucracy, the *Amtskirche*, as the Germans put it, needs to be made both credible and effective by transparency, accountability and decentralisation. As everyone knows, after an earthquake you must build differently, otherwise the same destruction will strike again.

CONCLUSION

Sometimes people wonder what St Paul looked like. We seem to know him already from the painting tradition which is remarkably consistent – or conservative – over many centuries. The earliest known portrait of Paul seems to be the one found in the Catacombs of St Thecla, on the Via Ostiense in Rome. It is a serious portrait, with a furrowed brow and a receding hair line. Later in the tradition, he acquires a sword, as a symbol of the word of God, 'Indeed, the word of God is living and active, sharper than any two-edged sword, piercing until it divides soul from spirit, joints from marrow; it is able to judge the thoughts and intentions of the heart' (Heb 4:12).

There exists, however, a quite early description of Paul. This occurs in the *Acts of Paul and Thecla*, a work dating from the second half of the second century. In the *Acts*, we find traditions and legends about Paul's missionary activity. In particular, his association with a young woman called Thecla finds expression in a series of episodes. In general, scholars would doubt the usefulness of the *Acts* with respect to the missionary activity of the historical Paul. Rather, this document, very interesting in itself, tells us about second century attitudes towards asceticism, religious enthusiasm and credulity. Nevertheless, it does contain a purported description of the Apostle, as follows:

> A certain man, by name Onesiphorus, hearing that Paul had come to Iconium, went out to meet him with his children Silas and Zeno, and his wife Lectra, in order that he might entertain him: for Titus had informed him what Paul was like in appearance: for he had not

seen him in the flesh, but only in the spirit. He went along the road to Lystra, and stood waiting for him, and kept looking at the passers by according to the description of Titus. *He saw Paul coming, a man small in size, bald-headed, bandy-legged, well-built, with eyebrows meeting, rather long-nosed, full of grace.* For sometimes he seemed like a man, and sometimes he had the countenance of an angel.

Acts of Paul and Thecla 1:3

Sometimes this is taken to be historical because it is not seen as flattering. However, the value of such descriptions becomes apparent when we realise that each feature had at the time a conventional interpretation. Pliny, in his *Natural History 11.275-6*, writes:

> When the *forehead* is large it indicates that the mind beneath it is sluggish; people with a small *forehead* have a nimble mind, those with a round forehead an irascible mind ...

When people's *eyebrows* are level this signifies that they are gentle, when they are curved at the side of the nose, that they are stern, when bent down at the temples that they are mockers, when entirely drooping, that they are malevolent and spiteful.

If people's *eyes* are narrow on both sides, this show them to be malicious in character; eyes that have fleshy corners on the side of the nostrils show a mark of maliciousness; when the white part of the eyes is extensive, it conveys an indication if impudence; eyes that have a habit of repeatedly closing indicate unreliability. Large *ears* are a sign of talkativeness and silliness.

So, in brief, we may decode the description as follows:

> Small in stature: that is, nimble, lively because the blood has a short trip around the body;

Bald-headed: a mark of humanity, as distinct from animal.

Bandy-legged: grounded, earthed, realistic.

Well-built: energetic.

Eyebrows meeting: gentle.

Long-nosed: of royal or noble lineage.

Full of grace: the gift from God which shaped Paul.

In a word, under the guise of a description of the outer person, we are furnished with a summary of the inner person. If we leave aside the appearance and look only at the interpretation, it turns out that the interpretation is not at all wide of the mark. Paul was indeed amazingly nimble, certainly in mind, probably also in body. He does come across as very human indeed, with a highly realistic and grounded appraisal of the world and its inhabitants. While he can be fierce, his desire is to be gentle, which he mostly is. The tribe of Benjamin was no mean lineage; a hint of family nobility alerts us to the astonishing nobility of spirit exhibited in the letters. And surely, he was graced by God, full of grace, a receiver of grace and a gracious giver of all he had himself received.

In the course of this study we have encountered this passionate visionary through a variety of lenses and using the seven undisputed letters. Throughout his relatively long life, he was always a man of faith and energy, before and after this 'turning'. His mind is penetrating – never taking issues on the surface but thinking deeply about the real issues at stake. He loves his communities and respects them enough to give always his most profound, sometimes difficult, theology. A man of prayer, whose relationship to Christ is there for all to see, even when he is cautious about special religious experiences. His physical energy, the immense journeys, the suffering, the joys, all speak of someone on fire, incandescent with the Good News. Paul the earliest theologian of the New Testament may very well have been also the greatest. Of him we may say he truly became what he proclaimed, so that he could say without fear of contradiction or even a hint of boasting: imitate me. From such a one, we can surely learn today. Even at the end of his life, he lifts us up with his humanity, his courage, his faith and his vision.

> Not that I have already obtained this or have already reached the goal; but I press on to make it my own, *because Christ Jesus has made me his own.* Beloved, I do not consider that I have made it my own; but this one thing I do: forgetting what lies behind and straining forward to what lies ahead, I press on toward the goal for the prize of the heavenly call of God in Christ Jesus (Phil 3:12-15).

Amen.

Appendix

PAUL AND INCLUSION: RACISM TODAY[1]

Along with human rights and ecology, racism, latent and overt, is one of *the* moral and religious challenges of this moment in our history. The manner in which we receive people from different countries and cultures tests not only our humanity but our Christianity. More often than not, we are discovering ourselves to be other than we would like to appear. At such a time, thoughtful religious people have the right to look to their foundational texts for guidance and inspiration.

It will be of interest to look at a single instance in the New Testament where the issue of welcoming the outsider arises, first to see what the response was then, and second to see if the response to that crisis might offer us guidance and encouragement for today. I want to take Christianity's first interpreter, Paul, and see how he responds to a perceived crisis in the Roman Christian community to which he wrote his longest letter, that to the Romans.

1. An earlier version of this chapter appeared as 'There is No Distinction – Inclusion in Paul' in *Responding to Racism: A Challenge and a Task for the Catholic Community*, Irish Commission for Justice and Peace, 2001, pp. 13–31.

    This chapter is offered as a 'non-religious' reading of Romans, touching on a great issue of concern today, racism. One of the ways in which the biblical text can be enabled to speak today is by comparison with contemporary issues, leading to a kind of 'parallel reading'. This reflection attempts to extract a teaching on universal inclusion of the other, a teaching which is based on faith realities, but which can be expressed in another not specifically Christian language. In this paper, there is a certain repetition of elements treated earlier in the chapters of the book. It seemed, however, better to include this text as an appendix so as to avoid duplication and thus retain the integrity of the reflection, while indicating the different character of the approach.

This examination will undertake three stages of argument, with three corresponding papers: a brief description of events in Rome just before the letter was written; an analysis of Paul's advice across the entire letter; and an attempt to correlate the issues and principles of today with the issues and principles of 2,000 years ago, and so to illuminate the present with the light of the past.

ANCIENT ROME AND ROMAN CHRISTIANS

Ancient Corinth had been a beautiful and vibrant city known for business acumen, educational possibilities and religious shrines. As is the nature of these things, the markets and the shrines are still there to be visited. Corinth at the time had a particular character – it was a largely Latin-speaking city in Greece, with a population of between 80–100,000. There were no censuses in those days, but based on housing and water supply, the size of the city can be approximately calculated. There are, of course, no churches as such from the period of Paul to be seen in Corinth. Instead the church, the Christian assembly, met in the houses of the wealthy who had space to accommodate guests. Even so, the largest *urban* gathering of Corinthian Christians would be about fifty persons. It seems clear that when Paul is writing to the Corinthians, he is not writing to *the* Corinthians, but to those few Corinthians who happened at the same time to be Christians. And even then, he writes to them as they meet in smaller groups. They seem to have come from the lower end of society at the time, because Paul writes: 'Consider your own call, brothers and sisters: not many of you were wise by human standards, not many were powerful, not many were of noble birth' (1 Cor 1:26).

Something similar may be said of the Roman Christians. The letter to the Romans was not proclaimed from the forum of Caesar, but read privately in some house or even flat belonging to a member of one of the Christian assemblies or house churches. Just as in the case of the Corinthians, we can ask what Rome was like and who the Roman Christians at that time were.

Rome at that period was the capital of the largest empire thus far seen. It was a highly cosmopolitan city, where Greek was widely spoken, as well, of course, as Latin. The Roman Empire had an estimated fifty to eighty million people in the countries and in the thousand or so cities under its control. A middle range city of the period would have had about 50,000 inhabitants. Rome was exceptional, with a population at this time of about one million people, about the size of Dublin today. There had been nothing quite like it before. In spite of its great size, still about 90 per cent of the subjects of the empire lived on the land. Within the whole population, about 20 per cent were slaves and about 10 per cent were Jews.

THE POLITICAL SITUATION AT THE TIME

Claudius became emperor on AD 24 January 41. He became emperor in an unusual way: the praetorians plucked him from his hiding place (apparently behind a curtain in the palace) and made him emperor. His fourth wife Agrippina, who was also his niece, arranged for his death by poison on 13 October 54, to facilitate the accession of her son. From a Jewish point of view, Claudius was an enlightened emperor and the Jewish historian Josephus tells us that he gave the Jews throughout the empire a guarantee that they could practise their religion 'without let or hindrance' (Josephus, Ant 19.290). However, in his *Lives of the Caesars*, Suetonius writes (Claudius 25.4): 'Since the Jews constantly made disturbances at the instigation of Chrestus, [Claudius] expelled them from Rome.' His expulsion of 'Jews' from Rome is apparently confirmed by Acts 18:2, where we read:

> There he found a Jew named Aquila, a native of Pontus,
> who had recently come from Italy with his wife Priscilla,
> because Claudius had ordered all Jews to leave Rome.
> Paul went to see them.

The next time we hear of the followers of 'Chrestus' in official documents is in the time of Nero, just after the city was burned. Nero (54–68) succeeded his stepfather Claudius on the demise of the latter. Nero did persecute the Christians, especially after the burning of Rome 18 July 64, but eventually found himself without support and took his own life.

Again, in his *Lives of the Caesars* (Nero 16), Suetonius mentions the Christians as a 'class of men given to a new and mischievous superstition'. It is interesting to note that he calls the religion a 'new' superstition and seems not to confuse it, as the earlier citation had done, with Judaism. This distinction is even clearer in the *Chronicle* (2:29) of Suplicius Severus. Nero had been blamed for the fire in Rome and tried to deflect blame by punishing the Christians who by now had become 'very large'. The same early example of spin doctoring is mentioned by Tacitus (Annals 15:44), who writes with a bracing disregard for political correctness:

> But all human efforts, all the lavish gifts of the emperor, and the propitiations of the gods did not banish the sinister belief that the conflagration was the result of an order. Consequently, to get rid of the report, Nero fastened the guilt and inflicted the most exquisite tortures on a class hated for their abominations, called Christians by the populace. Christus, from whom the name had its origin, suffered the extreme penalty during the reign of Tiberius at the hands of one of our procurators, Pontius Pilatus, and a most mischievous superstition thus checked for the moment, again broke out not only in Judaea, the first source of the evil, but even in Rome, where all things hideous and shameful from every part of the world find their centre and become popular.

The texts from the time of Nero tell us that by his time Christians had become distinguishable from Jews, because by now their membership had grown, and disliked by the general public they can easily be used as scapegoats. How did that development take place?

A scholarly hypothesis suggests the following possible sequence, which might help us to understand the letter to the Romans. Initially, as common sense would suggest and the documents apparently support, Christianity was essentially a Jewish phenomenon in Rome, and, although Christian, still retained a markedly Jewish identity. To cope with some civil disorder, Claudius felt obliged to expel the Jewish community from Rome and, of course, among them those Jews who were Christians. The subsequent vacuum in the Christian community allowed the Gentile Christians to come to prominence and take up leadership roles. This led to a certain weakening of the Jewish identity of the group. Eventually, the expulsion was relaxed and when the Jewish Christians returned they found themselves unable to reassert their influence in the community. The community was then divided along ethnic, and one might say religious, lines. It is, then, to this fractured community that Paul writes.

This is an attractive hypothesis. However, Claudius surely never expelled *all* the estimated 40–50,000 Jews in Rome. At least, there is no mention of it in Jewish sources of the period. He may very well have expelled people from the troublesome individual synagogues, especially Christian Jews, who were causing trouble. Synagogues were the essential organisational unit and it would have made more sense simply to expel the troublesome Jews-who-had-become-Christians, perhaps even a whole synagogue, rather than some blanket expulsion of *all* the Jews. In any case, as noted above, Claudius was otherwise known for a policy of clemency towards the Jews.

This much can be said. On balance, when you read the whole letter, Paul is dealing with a situation in which the Jewish part of the community is being devalued. This is why he starts with the Gentiles. This is why he so movingly expresses his concern for those of his own flesh. This is also why the sharpest threat in Romans is directed to the Gentiles. The challenge facing Paul in Romans is to show the two elements in the community how they belong to each other, how their basic identity is the same, and how their differences can be tolerated.

He does this by his teaching on faith, justification and the relative significance of Judaism for Gentiles.

Lastly, it is interesting that Paul writes to the Romans in Greek. It probably indicates that not only were the Jewish Christians not native Romans, neither were the Gentile Christians. In all likelihood, Christianity appealed to that part of the population which had nothing much to lose, either socially or economically, by becoming Christians, i.e. slaves and Jews. Paul could have repeated to the Romans what he said to the Corinthians: 'Consider your own call, brothers and sisters: not many of you were wise by human standards, not many were powerful, not many were of noble birth.' (1 Cor 1:26)

In a word, Paul is writing not to the imperial capital, to 'the Romans', but to those relatively few residents of Rome, most likely non-natives, who had become Christians. Within them is an ethnic and religious division which touches the core of Paul's Gospel: Jews and Christians belong together without the burden of the Law. He writes to them to offer not only practical advice but a theological approach which might allow them to set aside their mutual mistrust and hostility.

THE LETTER TO THE ROMANS

Paul admits towards the end of the letter to the Romans that he has expressed himself 'rather boldly'. There is a note of diffidence, somewhat unusual in Paul, at the opening and closing parts of the letter. There are two reasons for this. First of all, it is, on the face of it, a begging letter – Paul needs lodgings en route to Spain. Second, unlike all the other letters, Romans was written to a community that Paul did not found, and so he cannot claim a particular fatherly authority, as, for example, with the Corinthians. Not only had he not founded the community, he had never even been there. But don't let the diffidence fool you. Paul writes in full possession of his powers and sets out a strong and powerful argument to the Romans. Without burdening the text with unnecessary argument and detail, I think the letter to the Romans may be mapped as follows.

Apart from the usual beginning and ending in a letter, and using some of the categories of classical rhetoric, Romans can be structured as follows:

Verses	Term	Topic
1:8-15	Introduction	Reasons for coming to Rome.
1:16-17	Thesis	Justification by faith for Jews and Gentiles.
1:18–4:35	Proof 1	Neither Gentile nor Jew can claim any moral superiority – both stand equally in need of God's help in Christ.
5–8	Proof 2	In the light of all we receive in Christ, there is not distinction between Jews and Gentiles.
9–11	Proof 3	The respective roles of Jews and Gentiles in the history of salvation.
12:1–15:6	Proof 4	How Jews and Gentile could live together in harmony, tolerating differences.
15:7-33	Conclusion	Reasons for coming to Rome.

The theological tradition has for historical reasons (the Reformation and the Counter-Reformation) laid great emphasis on 1–4 and 5–8, dealing as they do with original sin and with grace. Equally for historical reasons 9–11 have been neglected, because in pre-ecumenical times, no Christian tradition has much use for a text that spoke of mutual belonging of Jews and Christians. These are the great theological sections in the letter. But the goal of all these considerations is peaceful cohabitation and this is what we finally arrive at in 12–15, with Paul's aim in writing to influence not only the thinking but the behaviour of the Roman Christians. Again, because of the theological tradition, no pre-ecumenical Christian tradition made these chapters the highpoint of the letter. These final chapters deal with principles and issues, conflict and tolerance in the Roman community. Building on the foundations of the previous chapters, Paul is able to propose solutions and resolutions which are not plucked out of the air, but grounded firmly in a subtle theology, the basis of which is that in Christ both Gentiles and Jews belong to each other. In my mind there is no doubting that the last section of the argument, 'life in the community', is Paul's point of arrival, where all the arguments finally come to a practical application and touch the living concerns of the community. It seems to be a lot of trouble to have taken, but the application needs a carefully thought-out, penetrating analysis before the advice can make sense, let alone be welcomed. In the last section from 12–15, we find the repeated call to acceptance and tolerance:

> For by the grace given to me I say to everyone among you not to think of yourself more highly than you ought to think, but to think with sober judgement, each according to the measure of faith that God has assigned. (Rom 12:3)

> We have gifts that differ according to the grace given to us: prophecy, in proportion to faith; ministry, in ministering; the teacher, in teaching; the exhorter, in exhortation; the giver, in generosity; the leader, in diligence; the compassionate, in cheerfulness.
> Let love be genuine; hate what is evil, hold fast to what is good; love one another with mutual affection; outdo one another in showing honour. (Rom 12:6-10)

> Welcome those who are weak in faith, but not for the purpose of quarrelling over opinions. (Rom 14:1)

> Why do you pass judgement on your brother or sister? Or you, why do you despise your brother or sister? For

we will all stand before the judgement seat of God. For it is written, 'As I live, says the Lord, every knee shall bow to me, and every tongue shall give praise to God'. So then, each of us will be accountable to God. (Rom 14:10-12)

Welcome one another, therefore, just as Christ has welcomed you, for the glory of God. (Rom 15:7)

Unlike many modern preachers, Paul does not want simply to exhort, but to persuade, to give good grounds for believing his advice and taking it to heart. Hence the sound foundation which he lays for this advice. Broadly speaking, in the first three stages of the argument are the following steps: (1) All have sinned, 'there is no distinction'; (2) All have equally received, forming 'a large family'; (3) Jews and Greeks need each other, 'there is no distinction'; (4) Practical advice on how to live together. We look briefly at each section.

Proof 1 – All are in need

Paul begins by describing the moral catastrophe of paganism, in language that reflects a genuine, if conventional, Jewish abhorrence. It is an interesting starting point. To hear it as a Gentile must have lead to an ambivalent reaction: from all this you have been converted and yet it remains your past – this is where you come from. To hear it as a Jew would be gratifying – at last someone to put the Gentiles in their place. Like all such moments of gratification in Paul, it doesn't last. Paul begins by praising the Jews:

But if you call yourself a Jew and rely on the law and boast of your relation to God and know his will and determine what is best because you are instructed in the law, and if you are sure that you are a guide to the blind, a light to those who are in darkness, a corrector of the foolish, a teacher of children, having in the law the embodiment of knowledge and truth, you, then, that teach others, will you not teach yourself? While you preach against stealing, do you steal? (Rom 2:17-21)

Having attacked one side, he now attacks the other. His question in 3:1 is given an apparently positive answer:

> Then what advantage has the Jew? Or what is the value of circumcision? Much, in every way. For in the first place the Jews were entrusted with the oracles of God. (Rom 3:1-2)

But this 'Much, in every way' is faint praise and a fuller reply is given in 3:9:

> What then? Are we any better off? No, not at all; for we have already charged that all, both Jews and Greeks, are under the power of sin …

He takes a great rhetorical risk here – the risk of insulting both audiences, reminding them of things they would much rather not recall. The risk is compensated for in two ways. First of all, insult is a way of holding people's attention, which is essential for communication. But you have to watch out for the law of diminishing returns. Second, he has destabilised both groups equally. It may have the effect of uniting them against him, but at least he shows no favouritism!

Having destabilised both groups, he presents the core of his argument, 3:21-24, where all the language of the thematic verses 1:16-17 is re-used. The significance of this 'no distinction' is then defended by the well-known argument from Abraham, an argument which is appealing to both groups in the community.

But now, apart from law, the righteousness of God has been disclosed, and is attested by the law and the prophets, the righteousness of God through faith in Jesus Christ for all who believe.

For there is no distinction, since all have sinned and fall short of the glory of God; they are now justified by his grace as a gift, through the redemption that is in Christ Jesus (Rom 3:21-24).

Proof 2 – All have received

In the second proof, there is a notable shift in language. The use of first person plural verbs ('we') across the letter is revealing: thirteen times in chapters 1–4, forty-eight times in chapters 5–8, five times in chapters 9–11 and eighteen times in chapters 12:1–15:13. This statistic gives an idea of what is happening in 5–8. Having undermined both sides of the community equally, Paul draws their attention to what unites them and what they have in common. Interestingly, there is no single statement that this is what they/we all have in common. It seems that just the very list has its own impact. It is a very Christ-centred proof, which takes us before Abraham to Adam.

What they have in common makes an impressive list, which respects the chronological sequence of their experience: first of all, he begins in the present with a description of the experience of faith of all who are in Christ. But he soon leaves the present aside to take us through what appears to be an account of salvation in chronological sequence: Christ, in his death and resurrection, reversed the deed of Adam; the Christian's entry into that reality through baptism, with the ethical consequences of having to live the same kind of life Christ lived; the common experience of moral dilemmas and difficulties, ending with a cry which is true of all human beings: 'Wretched man that I am! Who will rescue me from this body of death?' (Rom 7:24); faced again with the human dilemma of powerlessness, Paul's description of the gift of the spirit – experienced in Christian prayer as we cry out Abba, Father; the gift of the spirit who helps us when we do not know what to pray for; and finally Paul's turn to the future with unshakeable hope. From chapters 5–8 we move from Adam to the end of time, and the Christian's place in the overall scheme.

At no point in this argument does he repeat the idea that there is no distinction, but it is implied in the immense gifts they share as

Christians in the one community of faith. The points made here lay a foundation for the practical advice in chapters 12 and 14, when he deals with the community using the image of a body, again, with an implied argument that if this is all we have in common, then the divergences of practices are tolerable in comparison.

Proof 3 – The roles of Jews and Gentiles in God's vision

The third proof of the letter is the most emotional and intense, because in chapters 9–11 Paul speaks of his profound attachment to his own people and his pain at their substantial rejection of the messiah, as he sees it. The intensity is not only emotional. Paul faces a great theological dilemma: did God change his mind? Has the covenant been rescinded? Is their 'downfall' consistent with scripture? His teaching on this is difficult for us today. I suspect it was difficult also in Paul's day, but at least he is not afraid to bite the theological bullet. He thinks that in God's plan, Jews and Gentiles belong to each other – for this he uses the image of an olive tree and the grafting of a wild olive shoot on to the natural plant. He thinks the fact that most Jews did not recognise Jesus as the Christ opened an opportunity which was then used by God to extend salvation to all the human race, without an ethnic pre-condition:

> Just as you were once disobedient to God but have now received mercy because of their disobedience, so they have now been disobedient in order that, by the mercy shown to you, they too may now receive mercy. (Rom 11:30-31)

Nevertheless, Jews and Gentiles belong together, because God is always faithful, and eventually there will be a re-grafting of the original plant. He writes:

> For if you have been cut from what is by nature a wild olive tree and grafted, contrary to nature, into a

cultivated olive tree, how much more will these natural branches be grafted back into their own olive tree. (Rom 11:24)

Proof 4 – Finally, some practical advice

In the last proof of the argument, Paul arrives at the point of concrete application. This is the nub of the matter and is the heart of the letter, the moment when he wishes to influence not only their ideas, but also their behaviour. In different ways and for different reasons, Gentiles feel superior to Jews and Jews feel superior to Gentiles. Paul has looked at the human condition of Gentiles and Jews without Christ. He has recounted what Jews and Gentiles share in Christ. Finally, he shows historically how they belong together, with the result that there cannot be any destabilising sense of superiority. On the contrary, there should be a certainty about essentials and tolerance in regard to inessentials. Paul has laid the groundwork of his exhortation in the theological proofs from 1 to 3. Because of what he said there, he hopes the Roman Christians, both Jews and Gentiles, will manage not just to receive well and even to tolerate, but be able to love and treasure the variety. This comes to expression in the exhortations we have already seen about welcoming each other and so forth. But it comes to particular expression in two others moments.

The first of these is the image of the body. The body as a metaphor was a standard image taken from Stoic philosophy and used elsewhere by Paul himself in 1 Corinthians, where he also faced a divided community. The image of the body comes early in this argument:

> For as in one body we have many members, and not all the members have the same function, so we, who are many, are one body in Christ, and individually we are members one of another. We have gifts that differ according to the grace given to us: prophecy, in proportion to faith; ministry, in ministering; the

teacher, in teaching; the exhorter, in exhortation; the giver, in generosity; the leader, in diligence; the compassionate, in cheerfulness. (Rom 12:4-8)

The second moment is where he invites the more mature to forego something of their legitimate freedom simply in order to be loving towards the less advanced:

We who are strong ought to put up with the failings of the weak, and not to please ourselves. (Rom 15:1)

It is a high moral code, being a particular example of the love command of the New Testament. It is illuminating to see what kind of difficulties have arisen in the Roman community, and the tone of the reply reveals mild exasperation:

Some believe in eating anything, while the weak eat only vegetables. Those who eat must not despise those who abstain, and those who abstain must not pass judgement on those who eat; for God has welcomed them. Who are you to pass judgement on servants of another? It is before their own lord that they stand or fall. And they will be upheld, for the Lord is able to make them stand. Some judge one day to be better than another, while others judge all days to be alike. Let all be fully convinced in their own minds. Those who observe the day, observe it in honour of the Lord. Also those who eat, eat in honour of the Lord, since they give thanks to God; while those who abstain, abstain in honour of the Lord and give thanks to God. (Rom 14:2-6)

APPLICATION TODAY

We have looked at a concrete case in early Christianity and seen by what principles the difficulties of living together could be resolved.

What use is the consideration of these problems in a community remote in time and culture from ours? Can these texts speak to us today?

There are two ways in which we can draw inspiration from this text today, the first as believers and the second as human beings.

(i) In a faith perspective

For us, as believers, Paul's vision of a new humanity based on Christ is indeed a challenge. Paul has a powerful dream, which undergirds and motivates his entire apostolate. Something happened in Christ which means that the distinction into races and nations no longer matters before God and therefore before us. This is anything but abstract. For instance, it means that Paul organises the Jerusalem collection so that the impoverished Christians in Judaea might receive from the relatively well-off believers in, for instance, Corinth. Even more, his travelling is done to spread this message as widely as possible throughout the then-known inhabited world. The centre of this conviction is Christ – primarily in his death and resurrection, but also in his ethical teaching of love as the fulfilment of the law.

> Owe no one anything, except to love one another; for
> the one who loves another has fulfilled the law. (Rom
> 13:8)

In these days of not only privatisation but also individualisation, the connection between belief in Christ and our attitude to others is often overlooked. But Paul puts it plainly:

> Welcome one another, therefore, just as Christ has
> welcomed you, for the glory of God. (Rom 15:7)

In a word, an ethical imperative follows a salvific indicative. This reality of Jesus both as saviour who includes all and as a teacher (and practitioner) of inclusive ethics is just as valid today as in the time of Paul. Just as in the time of Paul it was difficult to practice, likewise today. But that's the challenge. A Church that calls itself 'catholic' cannot exclude anyone. The attempt to separate 'real' life from so-called 'prayer' life is precisely the root of the problem. For some, it is convenient to allow the proper separation of Church and State to lead to an altogether improper separation of faith and politics.

(ii)   In a non-faith perspective

Another way of making scripture speak to our time is to make parallel observations. It is clear that in the case of racism in this country the issue is not two groups believing in the same religion having difficulty in living together, though some of the arrivals share Christianity and even Catholicism with us. That is interesting but cannot be the main plank of an ethics of inclusion in our society today.

We can, however, make parallel observations. Paul's appeal for inclusion and for mutual acceptance is part of his whole vision of a renewed and reconciled human race. Each of his arguments would have a parallel today.

For instance, the point Paul wants to arrive at is mutual welcome, acceptance and understanding, based on an awareness of different gifts, that would go beyond mere toleration to loving welcome as a secular parallel. In the secular world, it would be possible to argue that we should value different gifts, we should welcome each other, we should be tolerant and welcoming and loving. But should we? And why should we? Here we can parallel the arguments Paul uses.

In the first proof, Paul argues from a sense of shared humanity, described particularly in his case in terms of a shared human dilemma, experienced and named as sin. We are even more aware today of a shared humanity. Sometimes this is experienced as a dilemma, the constant search for happiness, justice, respect and equal rights. If the rights of one person are in practice being impugned, then in principle my rights are under threat. We cannot make distinctions of persons. We could go on to detail how the search for happiness, stability, health, family life and work marks all humanity and the stranger is simply the brother and sister not properly met.

In the second proof, Paul argues from shared gifts, in practical terms of shared faith, baptism, ethical behaviour, spiritual experience and hope. It is possible to build a parallel argument. As humans we have all received the gift of existence, a shared humanity, and the gift of the world, a shared home. We all have the same in-built restlessness of heart and in our different ways catch glimpses of God out of the corner of our eye. Even the variety of human approaches to life is both a risk and a gift. Morally, we are more aware then ever that our choices affect the whole inhabited world. And we experience, together, the dilemma of being forced to make choices, knowing that even our good choices will have unwanted side effects. This is not something we experience alone, nor something we can handle alone. Neither is technology *the* answer, because technology as such is ethically neutral. A new human spirituality, with values, perhaps even an explicit belief in God, can give the moral courage and vision to lift us beyond our generation and do our best for the generations yet unborn. We need a vision of hope for all of us, if there is to be a vision of hope for any of us. If this is so, how can we pretend we are alone?

Perhaps the most difficult step to parallel is the mutual belonging of Jews and Gentiles, which arose in a particular moment in Christian history. It is a relationship still in need of understanding and it is possible that Romans can help. But, for our purposes here, perhaps it could be re-read today in this way. It is a relationship which in the past involved the Gentiles being indebted to the Jews, the many being indebted, in effect, to the one, and the Jews being indebted to the Gentiles, the one to the many. Each cultural and ethnic unit has something to bring to the many. In that sense, a value is placed on what is local and what is characteristic and what is specific. For us in Ireland, for example, we are aware of our characteristic cultural, spiritual, historical and political identities. At the same time, the 'little Englander' mentality, not at all limited to the English, needs to be balanced, or rather counterbalanced and challenged by a familiarity with other cultures and by an openness to what is common to us all simply as human beings.

In a faith perspective	Lessons for all people of good will
1. Argument from shared humanity, especially in terms of a shared human dilemma experienced as sinfulness.	Argument from common humanity, especially in terms of a dilemma, experienced as the search for happiness and justice.
2. Argument from shared gifts, especially in terms of shared faith, baptism, ethical behaviour, spiritual experience and hope.	Argument from shared gifts, especially in terms of a shared humanity, perhaps including a belief in God, but certainly ethical behaviour, a 'spirituality' and a hope for this world.
3. Argument from the mutual belonging of Jews and Gentiles, acknowledging the different historical roles.	Argument from mutual belonging of all of us on the planet, acknowledging different histories and different cultures.
4. Exhortation to receive each other, to live as a body, to practice tolerance and aim for a love which goes beyond the passivity of merely tolerating.	Exhortation to receive each other, to value the different gifts, to be tolerant and even more welcoming and loving.

Just as Paul has to ground his exhortation to the Romans in a close analysis of what it means to be human, whether as Jew or as Gentile, and only then goes on to exhort, likewise today we have an exhortation to offer. But if it comes merely as exhortation, we will not be listened to. We have to ground our exhortation in a close analysis of what it means to be human, whether as Jew or Gentile, white or black, Christian or Muslim, rich or poor, theist or atheist. Only then will our ethical appeal have a chance to be heard.

A Jewish parable can help here. A rabbi and his students were discussing the Law and their attention was focused particularly on the issue of being able to pinpoint exactly when dawn has arrived. One student said, 'The light has dawned when you can look into the distance and distinguish individuals from trees.' 'No,' said the rabbi.

'The day has started when you can distinguish a person's features,' offered another student. 'No,' said the rabbi. So they asked him, 'When has the light dawned and the day truly begun?' The rabbi said, 'The day has dawned and the light has truly begun to shine when you can look on the face of any man and recognise your brother.'

The issue of shared community values, especially between Jews and Gentiles, is present in practically every layer of the New Testament traditions. In other words, although it looks fairly certain that Jesus himself preached inclusion, his followers still had difficulty in putting it into practice. This could be because he wasn't really that clear, or it could be because it was very hard to live the principles, or perhaps some combination. For whatever reason, a good deal of the New Testament faces the continued tension between Jewish identity and Gentile inclusion.

We have looked at one context, Rome, as a sample sounding to see how Christianity's earliest interpreter, Paul, took up the challenge of an ethnically divided community. I think his approach can help us in two ways. First, it tells us that exhortation alone is not enough. Paul presents a deeply thought-out case before he advises. Analysis and thought are needed. Second, he provides us with principles of 'no distinction', which are even more valid today than they were in his time. As believers, we need to hear the clear words of St Paul:

> For there is no distinction between Jew and Greek; the same Lord is Lord of all and is generous to all who call on him. (Rom 10:12)

SUGGESTED FURTHER READING

Ascough, Richard S., Cotton, Sandy, *Passionate Visionary: Leadership Lessons from the Apostle Paul,* Toronto: Novalis, 2005.

Badiou, Alain, *St Paul: The Foundation of Universalism,* Stanford: Stanford University Press, 2003.

Campbell, William S., *Paul and the Creation of Christian Identity,* London/New York: T&T Clark, 2006.

Dunn, James D.G., *The Cambridge Companion to St Paul,* Cambridge: CUP, 2003.

Gaventa, Beverly Roberts, *Our Mother Saint Paul,* Louisville/London: Westminster John Knox Press, 2007.

Gorman, Michael, *Reading Paul,* Milton Keynes: Paternoster, 2008.

Harrington, Daniel J., *Meeting St Paul Today: Understanding the Man, His Mission, and His Message,* Chicago: Loyola Press, 2008.

Hooker, Morna D., *Paul: A Short Introduction,* Oxford: Oneworld, 2003.

Horrell, D., *An Introduction to the Study of Paul* (Continuum Biblical Studies Series), London: Continuum, 2000.

Matera, Frank, *Strategies for Preaching St Paul,* Collegeville: The Liturgical Press, 2001.

Murphy-O'Connor, Jerome, *St Paul's Ephesus: Texts and Archaeology,* Collegeville: The Liturgical Press, 2008.

Murphy-O'Connor, Jerome, *Paul the Letter-Writer: His World, His Option, His Skills,* Collegeville: The Liturgical Press, 1995.

Murphy-O'Connor, Jerome, *St Paul's Corinth: Texts and Archaeology,* Collegeville: The Liturgical Press, 1990.

Roetzel, Calvin, *Paul: A Jew on the Margins,* Louiseville: Westminster John Knox Press, 2003.

Still, Todd D. (ed.), *Jesus and Paul Reconnected: Fresh Pathways into an Old Debate*, Grand Rapids: Eerdmans, 2007.

Witherup, Ronald D., *101 Question & Answers on Paul*, New York: Paulist Press, 2003.

Wright, N.T., *Paul in Fresh Perspective*, Minneapolis: Fortress, 2005.

INDEX OF BIBLICAL CITATIONS

Genesis
2
136

Deuteronomy
21:22-23
46, 53, 60
21:23
145

Job
Whole book
75

Psalms
37
69, 75
73
69, 75

Jeremiah
1:4-5
55, 66
29:4-7
144

Ezekiel
37
69

Daniel
Whole book
43, 69 (bis)

1 Maccabees
Whole book
43

2 Maccabees
Whole book
43, 69 (bis)
7
43

7:1-6
44

4 Maccabees
15-18
43

Matthew
10:9-10
110
14:3-12
20
23:8-12
147 fn 18
23:15
44

Mark
1:22
40
10:42-45
146
12:29-31
94

Luke
10:7
110
24:34
68

John
7:39
68
11:4
68
12:16
68
12:23
68
12:28
68
13:31-32
68

14:13
68
15:8
68
17
63
17:4
68
17:10
68

Acts
4:36 7
6
5:34-41
48
8:1-3
45
9:1-2
45
9:3-19
45
9:9-19
53
9:23-25
19
9:26-28
20
9:27
76
10:2
49
10:22
49
10:35
49
11:22
76
11:25
76
11:30
76
12:25–13:2
76

13:7
  76
13:16
  49
13:26
  49
13:42-43
  76
13:43
  49
13:46
  76
13:50
  48, 76
14:1
  76
14:12
  76
14:14
  76
14:20
  76
15
  83
15:2
  76
15:12
  76
15:22
  76
15:22-29
  26
15:25
  76
15:35-37
  76
15:36-39
  76
15:39
  76
16:14
  49
17:4
  49
17:17
  49
17:22-31
  29
18:2
  139, 155
18:7
  49
18:12-17
  21

22:1-21
  45, 53
22:3
  48
26:2-23
  45, 53

Romans
Whole letter
  23, 34, 131
1–4
  36, 95, 117, 140,
  142, 159, 163
1:1
  46
1:4
  46
1:5
  142 fn 9
1:6-8
  46
1:8
  142 fn 9
1:8-15
  92, 159
1:9-10
  117
1:11-12
  113
1:12
  142 fn 9
1:16-17
  142 fn 9, 159, 162
1:17-18
  66
1:18-32
  140
1:18–4:35
  159
2–4
  96
2:1
  140 fn 5
2:4
  144 fn 11
2:5
  66
2:16
  46
2:16-17
  142 fn 9
2:17
  139 fn 2
2:17-21
  162

2:1-24
  141
2:23
  139 fn 2
3:1-2
  142 fn 7, 162
3:2-3
  142 fn 9
3:9
  142 fn 8, 162
3:21-22
  117
3:21-24
  162, 163
3:21-26
  143
3:22
  142 fn 9, 143 fn 10
3:24
  144 fn 12
3:25-28
  142 fn 9
3:30-31
  142 fn 9
4:2
  139 fn 2
4:3
  142 fn 9
4:5
  142 fn 9
4:9
  142 fn 9
4:11-14
  142 fn 9
4:16-20
  142 fn 9
4:24
  46, 142 fn 9
5
  95
5-8
  36, 95, 100, 101, 117,
159, 163 (bis)
5:1-2
  142 fn 9
5:1-5
  91, 96, 101
5:2-3
  139 fn 2
5:5
  101
5:8
  101
5:11
  139 fn 2

6
95
6:5-11
72
6:8
142 fn 9
6:11
144 fn 12
6:23
144 fn 12
7
52, 95, 96
7:24
163
7:24-25
96
8
95, 96, 97, 100, 101, 102
8:1-2
96, 100, 144 fn 12
8:3-4
96
8:5-8
96
8:9-11
96, 97
8:11
46
8:18
97
8:18-19
66
8:19
97
8:21
105
8:22-23
71
8:24-25
98
8:26-28
98
8:28
101
8:28-30
99, 101
8:31-39
100
8:34
46
8:34-35
100
8:35
81, 82, 101

8:39
14, 101
8:39–9:1
144 fn 12
9–11
118, 159 (bis), 163, 164
9:1-3
84
9:30
142 fn 9
9:32-33
142 fn 9
10:4
142 fn 9
10:6
142 fn 9
10:8-11
142 fn 9
10:9
46 (bis)
10:11
142
10:12
117, 171
10:14
142 fn 9
10:16-17
142 fn 9
11:20
142 fn 9
11:24
165
11:30-31
164
12
164
12–15
159, 160
12:1–15:6
118, 159
12:1–15:13
36, 163
12:2
145 fn 13
12:3
142 fn 9, 160
12:4-5
118
12:4-8
166
12:5
144 fn 12
12:6
118, 142 fn 9

12:6-10
160
13:8
167
13:8-10
95
13:11
142 fn 9
14
164
14:1
160
14:1-2
142 fn 9
14:2-6
166
14:10-12
161
14:22-23
142 fn 9
15:1
166
15:7
161, 167
15:7-33
159
15:13
142 fn 9
15:17
144 fn 12, 161
15:23-24
107
16
136
16:3
144 fn 12
16:1-2
133
16:7
107, 144 fn 12
16:9-10
144 fn 12
16:25
66
16:26
142 fn 9

1 Corinthians
Whole letter
23, 34, 131, 165
1
17
1:2
144 fn 12
1:4
144 fn 12

1:4-9
  92
1:5-7
  93
1:7
  66
1:9
  142 fn 9
1:11-12
  115
1:11-13
  124
1:14-16
  24
1:18-24
  87
1:21
  142 fn 9
1:25
  146
1:26
  154, 158
1:26-27
  123
1:29
  139 fn 2
1:30
  144 fn 12
1:31
  139 fn 2
2:1-5
  146 fn 16
2:5
  142 fn 9
2:9
  71
2:10
  66
3:1
  144 fn 12
3:2
  24, 114
3:5
  142 fn 9
3:5-7
  115
3:13
  66
3:21
  139 fn 2
4:2
  142 fn 9
4:7
  139 fn 2

4:10
  144 fn 12
4:11-13
  81 (bis)
4:14
  46
4:15
  79, 115, 144 fn 12
4:16
  15
4:17
  142 fn 9, 144 fn 12
5:6
  139 fn 2
7
  131, 136
7:1-7
  132
7:25
  142 fn 9
9:6
  76
9:10-14
  111
9:15-16
  139 fn 2
9:17
  142 fn 9
10:13
  142 fn 9
10:16-17
  128
11
  135, 136
11:1
  15
11:3-16
  135
11:14-16
  136 (bis)
11:16
  136
11:17-22
  123, 124
11:18
  142 fn 9
11:19-21
  129
11:20-22
  127
11:23-26
  127
11:27-32
  128

11:33-34
  123, 127
12:3
  46
12:5-6
  139 fn 2
12:9
  142 fn 9
12:12-13
  129
13
  94
13:2
  142 fn 9
13:3
  139 fn 2
13:7
  142 fn 9
13:13
  101, 142 fn 9
14
  133
14:6
  66
14:18-19
  93
14:22
  142 fn 9
14:26
  66
14:29-38
  132
14:30
  66
15
  17, 24
15:2
  142 fn 9
15:3-5
  72
15:8
  53, 145
15:9
  45
15:11
  142 fn 9
15:14
  142 fn 9
15:17
  142 fn 9
15:18-19
  144 fn 12
15:22
  144 fn 12

15:31
  144 fn 12
15:35-36
  71
15:51-53
  67
15:57
  74
16:13
  142 fn 9
16:24
  144 fn 12

2 Corinthians
Whole letter
  23, 34, 37, 131
1–7
  79
1:3-11
  92
1:8-11
  84
1:14
  139 fn 2
1:18
  142 fn 9
1:19-20
  74
1:24
  142 fn 9
2:4-6
  106
2:10
  144 fn 12
2:12-13
  84
2:14
  144 fn 12
2:17
  144 fn 12
3:14
  144 fn 12
4:8-10
  81 (bis)
4:13
  142 fn 9
4:13-15
  18
5:7
  101, 142 fn 9
5:12
  139 fn 2
5:16-21
  80

5:17
  144 fn 12
5:19
  144 fn 12, 145
6:3-10
  81, 82
6:11-12
  80
6:11-13
  37
6:15
  142 fn 9
7:2
  37
7:2-4
  80
7:9-10
  144 fn 11
7:9-11
  76, 142, 144
7:14
  139 fn 2
8:7
  142 fn 9
9:2-3
  139 fn 2
10:8
  139 fn 2
10:9-10
  83
10:10
  16
10:13
  139 fn 2
10:15
  142 fn 9
10:15-17
  139 fn 2
11:12
  39 fn 2
11:16
  139 fn 2
11:16-23
  85
11:18
  139 fn 2
11:23-29
  81, 82
11:30
  139 fn 2
11:32-33
  19
12
  14, 54, 83

12:1
  66, 139 fn 2
12:1-7
  85
12:2
  144 fn 12
12:2-5
  68
12:5-6
  139 fn 2
12:7
  66
12:9
  139 fn 2
12:10
  81, 82, 146
12:19
  144 fn 12
12:21
  144 fn 11
13:5
  142 fn 9

Ephesians
Whole letter
  23, 38
2:14
  139 fn 3
2:14-16
  61
5:22-31
  130

Galatians
Whole letter
  23, 131
1
  53
1:1
  46
1:6
  144 fn 12
1:6-9
  78
1:11-12
  65
1:11-18
  54
1:11-24
  53
1:12
  66
1:13
  45

DO WE STILL NEED ST PAUL?

1:13-17
  90, 145
1:15-16
  14
1:15-17
  65
1:16
  66
1:18-20
  20
1:22
  45, 63, 144 fn 12
1:23
  142 fn 9
2
  83
2:1
  76
2:2
  66
2:3-5
  94
2:4
  144 fn 12
2:7
  142 fn 9
2:9
  76
2:13
  76 (bis)
2:15-21
  61, 86
2:16
  142 fn 9, 143 fn 10
2:17
  144 fn 12
2:19-20
  147
2:19-21
  145 fn 15
2:20
  4, 55, 66, 142 fn 9, 144 fn 12
3
  136
3:2
  142 fn 9
3:2-5
  94
3:5-9
  142 fn 9
3:11-12
  142 fn 9
3:13-14
  46, 60

3:14
  142 fn 9, 144 fn 12
3:22
  143 fn 10
3:22-26
  142 fn 9
3:23
  66
3:24
  143 fn 10
3:26
  143 fn 10, 144 fn 12
3:27-29
  124, 131
3:28
  106, 144 fn 12
4:12
  15
4:12-15
  81, 83
4:12-20
  79
5:1
  106
5:2-6
  78
5:5-6
  142 fn 9
5:6
  144 fn 12
5:11-12
  79
5:14-15
  95
5:22
  142 fn 9
5:22-23
  106
5:22-26
  94
6:4
  139 fn 2
6:10
  142 fn 9
6:13-14
  139 fn 2

Colossians
Whole letter
  23, 38
3:11
  124
3:18-25
  130

Philippians
Whole letter
  23, 131
1:1
  144 fn 12
1:3-11
  91
1:8
  144 fn 12
1:12-14
  146 fn 17
1:13
  144 fn 12
1:25
  142 fn 9
1:26
  139 fn 2, 144 fn 12
1:27
  142 fn 9
1:29
  142 fn 9
2:1
  144 fn 12
2:5
  144 fn 12, 145
2:9
  67
2:16
  139 fn 2
2:17
  142 fn 9
3:3
  139 fn 2, 144 fn 12
3:4-6
  45
3:7-11
  50
3:7-15
  73
3:9
  142 fn 9, 143 fn 10
3:10-15
  147
3:12-15
  152
3:14
  144 fn 12
3:15
  66
4:7
  144 fn 12
4:19
  144 fn 12
4:21
  144 fn 12

1 Thessalonians
Whole letter
  23, 24, 25, 31, 131
1:1
  31
1:1-10
  92
1:2-3
  92
1:2-10
  31
1:3
  142 fn 9
1:4-5
  92
1:6
  15, 113
1:7-8
  142 fn 9
1:9-10
  31 (bis)
1:10
  46
2:1–3:12
  31
2:4
  142 fn 9
2:7-8
  112
2:8
  145 fn 14
2:10
  142 fn 9
2:13
  142 fn 9
2:14
  144 fn 12
2:17
  35
2:17-18
  25
2:17–3:5
  77
3:2
  142 fn 9
3:5-7
  142 fn 9
3:10
  142 fn 9
3:11-1
  92
4:1-12
  31
4:13–5:11
  31

4:14
  142 fn 9
4:16
  144 fn 12
5:3
  71
5:1-11
  67
5:8
  142 fn 9
5:12-13
  24, 107
5:12-27
  31
5:18
  144 fn 12
5:2
  142 fn 9
5:28
  31

2 Thessalonians
Whole letter
  23, 131
1:7
  66
2:3
  66
2:6
  66
2:8
  66
3:7
  15
3:9
  15

Philemon
Whole letter
  23, 131
4–7
  92
5–6
  142 fn 9
8
  144 fn 12
20
  144 fn 12
23
  144 fn 12

1 Timothy
Whole letter
  23, 38, 130
2:8-15
  130 (bis), 131, 132
5:1-2
  130
5:17-18
  111
6:1-2
  130

2 Timothy
Whole letter
  23, 38, 130

Titus
Whole letter
  23, 38, 130
2:1-10
  130
3:1
  130

Hebrews
2:14-18
  62
4:12
  149

2 Peter
3:15-16
  13
3:16
  109

Revelation
Whole book
  63
2:1-2
  66

INDEX OF NON-BIBLICAL CITATIONS

Act of Paul and Thecla
1:3
150

God is love (Benedict XVI)
1
18, 90

Chronicle (Sulpicius Severus)
2:29
156

That Nature is a Heraclitean Fire and of the comfort of the Resurrection (Gerard Manley Hopkins)
102

Didache
12:1-13:1
III

History (Tacitus)
Annals 15:44
156

Jewish Antiquities (Josephus)
Ant 18.5.1-3 §109-125
20
Ant 19.290
125

Letters (Pliny)
2:2
125

Lives of the Caesars (Suetonius)
Claudius 25:4
155

Nero
16, 126

Natural History (Pliny)
11:275-6
150